To Pat with much love from

~John~

See p. 164.

10/31/03

HISTORIC BUILDINGS
OF THE FRENCH QUARTER

FRENCH MARKET

V. VOGT

HISTORIC BUILDINGS
OF THE FRENCH QUARTER

LLOYD VOGT

PELICAN PUBLISHING COMPANY
Gretna 2002

The word "Pelican" and the depiction of a pelican are trademarks of
Pelican Publishing Company, Inc., and are registered in the
U.S. Patent and Trademark Office.

Library of Congress Cataloging-in-Publication Data

Vogt, Lloyd.
   Historic buildings of the French Quarter / Lloyd Vogt.
     p. cm.
   Includes bibliographical references.
   ISBN 1-56554-997-X (alk. paper)
    1. Architecture—Louisiana—New Orleans. 2. New Orleans (La.)—
Buildings, structures, etc. 3. Vieux Carré (New Orleans, La.)—Buildings,
structures, etc. I. Title.

NA735.N4 V64 2002
720'.9763'35—dc21

                                          2001059813

Page 42: *Ursuline Convent, courtesy Historic New Orleans Collection*
Page 68: *Merieult House railing, courtesy* Old New Orleans
Page 76: *Orue-Pontalba House railing, courtesy* Old New Orleans
Page 82: *Banque de la Louisiane railing, courtesy* Old New Orleans
Page 86: *Cabildo railing, courtesy* Old New Orleans
Page 140: *Victor David House railings, courtesy* Old New Orleans
Page 142: *Arsenal, courtesy* The Cabildo on Jackson Square
Page 144: *LaBranche Buildings, courtesy* Old New Orleans

Printed in China
Published by Pelican Publishing Company, Inc.
1000 Burmaster Street, Gretna, Louisiana 70053

This book is dedicated to all those who fought and defeated the proposed elevated riverfront expressway planned to run along the river and separate the French Quarter from its source, the Mississippi. Their foresight, wisdom, and dedication to a battle that lasted over twenty-six years prevented a monstrosity that would have destroyed the Quarter and any reasons for the current work.

To the following leaders of the fight: Richard O. Baumbach, Jr., William E. Borah, Raymond J. Boudreaux, former archbishop Philip M. Hannen, John W. Lawrence, William J. Long, Mark P. Lowrey, Mary Morrison, Martha G. Robinson, Edgar B. Stern, Jr., and to the many others who contributed, too many to name, our sincere thanks.

CONTENTS

ACKNOWLEDGMENTS

I would like to acknowledge with gratitude the following for their support, research assistance, and the sharing of their thoughts and ideas about this manuscript: Robert Heck, Jay Edwards, Reba Capers, William Borah, Ann Tucker, Caroline Capers, Kristina Neidballa, Geoff Coates, Bonnie Harris, Darren Vogt, Ian Vogt, Corlie Ohl, Peggy Landry, Heidi Hitter, and the staff of the Historic New Orleans Collection. I would also like to acknowledge the extremely valuable body of published research of Samuel Wilson and Jay Edwards.

Lloyd Vogt

INTRODUCTION

THE FRENCH QUARTER, NEW ORLEANS' historic center, is the most unique sixty-six square blocks in America. Designated as a national historic landmark in 1965, it is a place in which the lives of thousands of people of great cultural diversity have blended together, creating a unique community and a unique way of life. Their influence is still very much evident; their presence seems to linger in each courtyard and on each balcony. And while the individual cultures that created the Quarter have blended with one another, their essence remains, each having contributed to a uniqueness that defies rational explanation. Formally known as the *Vieux Carré*, and locally as the *Quarter*, it is a potpourri of sights, sounds, smells, and attitudes descendent of a bygone era, interacting for almost three hundred years to weave this vibrant tapestry.

The character of the Quarter derived from European tradition. It is a self-contained, self-sustaining community, combining living, working, dining, shopping, and recreation. Buildings of importance, such as churches and public buildings, are located facing the commons, where their importance can be properly announced and viewed. By contrast, buildings of less significance, such as houses, restaurants, bars, and shops, are designed to compliment and blend with one another, creating a streetscape in which the ensemble is more important than individual buildings.

The Quarter manifests an attitude of tolerance—an essential characteristic that has drawn the likes of Tennessee Williams and William Faulkner to live, work, and absorb the experience of everyday life, for here, the experience of everyday life seems to be magnified.

Bounded by the Mississippi River, Canal Street, Rampart Street, and Esplanade Avenue, the French Quarter is intrinsically tied to the river and its port, the highway from which this potpourri of cultures first set foot on these distant shores. Since there was very little cultural interaction between New Orleans and the rest of North America from the time of its colonization until the Louisiana Purchase in 1803, the Quarter more closely resembles a Caribbean port than an American city—the architecture, food, music, and lifestyle evolved during a time when the city's culture was more akin to the West Indies than to America.

The question often arises as to whether the character of the French Quarter is French or Spanish. While there are certain architectural characteristics that can be attributed to the French or Spanish culture in the New World colonies, the Quarter is more *Creole* than anything, for it was the French and Spanish Creoles, learning from their experiences in the West Indies, that created the Quarter's architectural uniqueness.

The term *Creole* requires explanation, since it has come to be used in many different ways. In New Orleans, its origin is tied to the French colony of Saint Domingue, where during the seventeenth and eighteenth centuries, *Creole* meant native-born, without reference to color. It was this tradition that took root in colonial Louisiana as early as the beginning of the French settlement at Mobile in the early 1700s (Tregle, Jr., 1992).

While there are many historic districts in America, no other seems to have remained as intact as the Quarter. The reason for this lies in the unique set of circumstances surrounding the Quarter's past. The typical process of colonial development begins with the founding of a settlement with temporary shelter, soon followed by stabilization with more substantial buildings—usually small, modest structures to house the newcomers. As the population increases, the smaller, insignificant structures are demolished to make way for larger structures. Thus, a successful, growing city continues to destroy and rebuild itself. This process has been responsible for the destruction of most of the historic areas in America and continues today in New Orleans in the central business district as well as other historic districts.

So why did this destructive process not occur in the Quarter? The Quarter experienced a series of events that allowed it to escape the ravages of growth and progress in the twentieth century, but more significantly, it experienced two devastating fires in the late 1700s that

accelerated those processes. While the great fires of 1788 and 1794 destroyed almost all of the city, the result was its rebuilding of more substantial buildings in a short period of time in order to house a population of about 5,000 left homeless. A process that normally would have taken a hundred years was accomplished in ten.

The circumstances by which the Quarter escaped destruction from demolition and rebuilding in the early twentieth century are also intriguing. By the end of the 1800s, the Quarter had fallen out of favor as a desirable place to live, and consequently, the process of destruction and reconstruction took place across Canal Street in the present-day central business district. The new high-rise technology being developed at the time (made feasible by electric elevators) made the existing two-, three-, and four-story buildings obsolete in areas where land was scarce, resulting in the mass destruction of these smaller buildings in city centers across America, and the replacement of them with mid-rise and high-rise structures and parking lots.

In the 1930s, when this process of demolition and reconstruction finally began to cross Canal Street into the Quarter, a number of wise New Orleanians became alarmed. Thanks to their wisdom, they influenced the city government to establish the Vieux Carré Commission to protect the historic character of the Quarter. It was the second historic district in America. Preservation efforts in the Quarter have continued since that time, guided and protected by the Vieux Carré Commission.

The research for this book was conducted through extensive literary research and on-site, local, regional, and international travel. The primary sources of information for the historic structures featured herein were The Historic New Orleans Collection, The Vieux Carré Commission, Sam Wilson, Jr.'s *A Guide to Architecture of New Orleans 1699-1959*, Leonard Huber's *Landmarks of New Orleans,* and Roulhac Toledano's *The National Trust Guide to New Orleans,* and are listed in the bibliography. Where deemed appropriate, entries from diaries and journals of those who actually experienced life in the colony are quoted—such as Iberville, Bienville, and Benjamin Latrobe—for it was felt that in many instances, their firsthand description was better than a contemporary interpretation.

Through the years, recognition of the Quarter's importance has grown not only locally, but also nationally and internationally, and the number of visitors increases year after year. It is the only city in the world where the three major cultures of France, Spain, and England played a major role in its development and where the evidence of each culture, while having blended through time, is still evident.

Places are an expression of a culture, and when one learns to *read* the Quarter, the cultures that influenced it come into focus; conversely, when one understands the cultures, the *place* comes into focus. People are intrinsically linked to their built environment—a *place* is the direct result of its inhabitants, its builders, and its governors. It represents the struggles for survival and the enrichment of everyday life experiences and manifests the dreams and aspirations of those it has embraced. People build cities; cities, in turn, build cultures.

This book is an attempt to tell the story of this very unique place through its architecture.

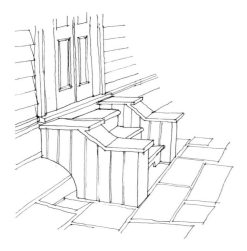

13

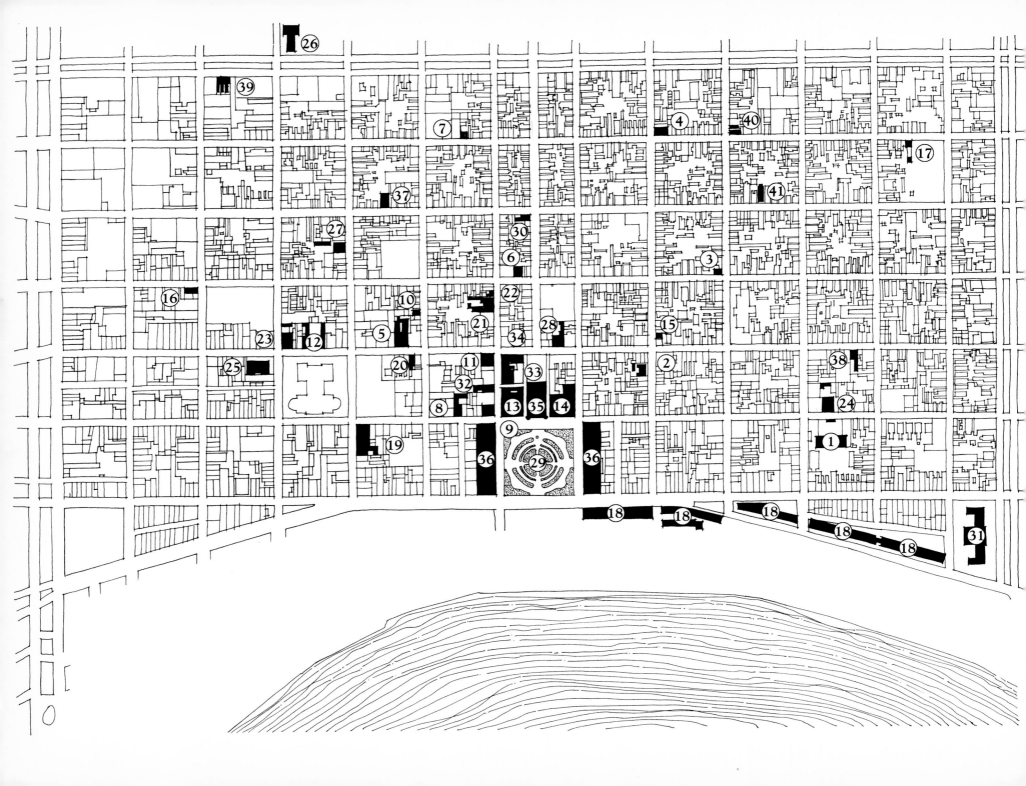

LEGEND

HISTORIC BUILDINGS
OF THE FRENCH QUARTER

THE NEW WORLD
Exploration & Colonization

NEW ORLEANS, LIKE OTHER EUROPEAN settlements in the New World, can best be understood by understanding the traditions of its founding colonists. In planning and building the city, the settlers of New Orleans utilized an assembly of cultural traditions, primarily from the three principal European powers of the seventeenth and eighteenth centuries: France, Spain, and England. Establishing a clear delineation, or determining which qualities of the city are uniquely French, Spanish, or English, has proven to be difficult. It has also been the source of much of the lively debate and critical discussion among students and historians of New Orleans.

The political boundaries defining the countries of Europe identified the inhabitants with a sovereign power, not necessarily with a homogeneous cultural tradition. Architectural traditions in eighteenth- and nineteenth-century Europe were more aligned by regional geography than political boundaries. Climate and the availability of natural resources for building played a larger role in forming these traditions than did nationality.

Thus, it is more constructive to view the origins of the building traditions imported to the New World in terms of three major regions of western Europe, rather than nations: southern Mediterranean, northern Mediterranean, and central Europe. Many of the building methods of these regions were first introduced by the Romans from 100 B.C. to 300 A.D., and at the time of the discovery and exploration of the New World, the Italian Renaissance was exerting tremendous influence throughout all of Europe.

While the basic forms of traditional housing at this time were similar throughout western Europe, roof pitches, construction materials, and techniques differed considerably from region to region. In the southern Mediterranean, including the hot, arid Andalusian region

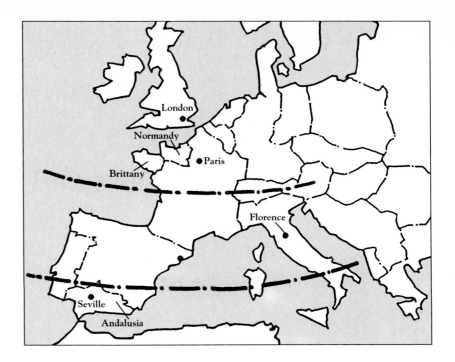

of Spain, traditions introduced by the Moors from North Africa included construction with stone or brick, stuccoed and coated with whitewash. The whitewashing tradition was as much functional as aesthetic, as it helped the buildings to reflect the heat of the Mediterranean sun. Roofs were flat and covered with flat clay tiles or slightly pitched, covered with barrel-clay tile.

Moving into the northern Mediterranean region, construction was primarily of stone, but roof pitches gradually increased. On the northeastern coast of Spain, the southern coast of France, and in northern Italy, roofs were typically pitched between twenty and thirty degrees, generally covered with barrel-clay tile. Continuing north into central Europe, stone and brick construction were common, while in villages near forests, timber framing with stone or brick infill also occurred frequently. Farther north, as a technique for shedding

19

rain and snow, roof pitches gradually increased, reaching approximately sixty degrees in northern France and England. Roofing materials include thatch, wood shingles, slate shingles, as well as clay tile.

All of these building traditions and techniques found a home in the New World, including New Orleans, where the unique climatic conditions and natural resources resulted in unique solutions and an equally unique architecture.

20

THE NEW WORLD COLONIES

The new world explorations of the fifteenth and sixteenth centuries originated in a period of unprecedented cultural, political, and social *excitement*.

The medieval era of European history, frequently referred to as the Dark Ages, was coming to an end. The intellectual, artistic, and economic awakening in Italy, which originated in Florence, was, by the fourteenth century, spreading across western Europe, ushering in a period of immense creativity and expanded cultural energy. It was an unprecedented period of growth, development, and innovation in all areas of European life and culture: art, architecture, literature, commerce, and politics. As the newly energized, European political states set out to explore and colonize new territories, it was with a spirit of pride, invincibility, heroism, and intense nationalism.

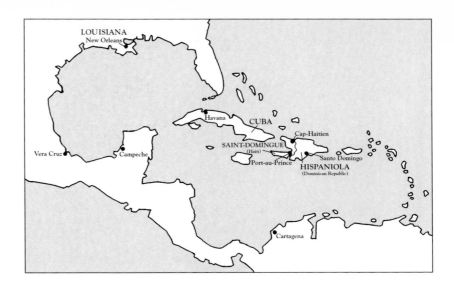

The Spanish

On October 12, 1492, after thirty-three days at sea, Christopher Columbus, an Italian under the patronage of Queen Isabella of Spain, made landfall on San Salvador in the West Indies. After coursing through the Bahamas, the northern coasts of eastern Cuba, and Hispaniola, he returned to Spain to announce his discovery of a new route to Asia.

Soon thereafter, Columbus returned to the West Indies to initiate the era of colonization. After a failed attempt in 1493 to establish a settlement on the northern coast of Hispaniola (the Dominican Republic), the first permanent colony, Santo Domingo, was founded on that same island by Columbus's brother Bartolomeo in 1496. In the years following, colonization increased drastically, as Spain set sail further westward to the mainland of the Americas in search of gold, silver, adventure, and a quick route to the Orient.

The Spanish founded colonies on the islands of the Greater Antilles: Cuba, Puerto Rico, and Jamaica. Gold was discovered on all but Jamaica, and a brief gold rush drew thousands of Spaniards. After approximately ten years of furious activity, the gold supply was exhausted, and colonists moved on in search of other gold deposits, leaving the islands all but abandoned. Since the Lesser Antilles had no gold, they were ignored.

Ignoring the superior harbor at Havana, the Spanish established Santiago on the southeast coast of Cuba as their new center of activity, and the search for wealth continued as they sailed westward, colonizing Mexico and Central and South America. In 1519 they established a port at Vera Cruz, Mexico, from which they traveled inland to capture the Aztec capital of Tenochtitlán in 1521, renaming it Mexico City, which was to become the capital of the empire of New Spain. In 1533, they established the port of Cartagena, Colombia, which would become the port of departure for ships leaving from South America. Vera Cruz was the point of departure from Mexico.

In Mexico and Peru, the Spanish finally found the wealth they were searching for, although it was mostly silver rather than gold. The treasure was loaded onto ships and delivered to Spain, increasing the country's wealth immensely. In response to raids by English and French pirates, the Spanish government established a convoy of

21

Spanish warships to escort the treasure-bearing fleets from the ports of Cartagena and Vera Cruz across the Atlantic to Seville in Andalusia.

While Santo Domingo remained the administrative capital of the Spanish Antilles, by the 1560s, Havana had become the most important port in the Spanish New World. Because of its strategic location in the Gulf Stream, the strongest ocean current in the world, it was the origin of the quickest route to Spain.

As Spain expanded its empire, planning principles were guided by the *Laws of the Indies (Recopilacion de Leyes de las Indias)*. Developed over a number of years, these principles were codified in 1573, and by 1681, in its final form, the Laws contained approximately 6,400 precepts, arranged in nine books that guided in minute detail the organization, activities, and the physical siting, layout, and design of Spanish colonial municipalities.

The Laws imposed a standard town plan for all new settlements, directing the colonists to integrate regional geographic factors (climate, wind direction, availability of water, soil quality, and suitability for defense) into the Spanish model. The size and shape of a central plaza was fixed, as well as the width and orientation of the streets, location of public buildings, and the division of blocks into lots. Streets were to be laid out in a strict grid pattern, a geometry originating in ancient Greece and first introduced in Spain by the Romans in the first century B.C.

The plan centered around the *plaza mayor*, the main plaza, fronting on which were the principal church, the *cabildo*, and the prison. The plaza created the focal point of the city—the center of political, military, ecclesiastical, commercial, and social activity. Dimensions for plazas were specific: rectangular with four corners aligned with the compass points; the minimum size was set at 200 by 300 feet with one side one-and-one-half times as long as the other. Two streets were to meet at right angles at each corner, and four more were to lead from the center of each side to facilitate an orderly procession of military parades. Buildings facing the plaza were to incorporate *portales*, or shaded arcades, for the convenience of merchants and pedestrians. In addition to housing municipal buildings, private palaces, shops, and market stalls, the plaza also served as a setting for military parades, fiestas, and public executions (Carley 1997).

The architecture in the Spanish colonies was first guided by engineers sent in to lay out the colony and construct the prominent buildings. At the time, the administrative seat of colonization was Seville in Andulusia (southern Spain). Consequently, the buildings constructed by the engineers were influenced by the traditions of that region, whose hot and arid climate was fortunately similar to that of the West Indies and Mexico. In Santo Domingo, they introduced the Andalusian patio house, combining symmetrical plans with simplified Isabelline and Mudéjar details, focused inward toward a central courtyard, which the Spanish called *patio*—the French courtyard.

The Spanish colonists were also, for the most part, coming from southern Spain. For their residences they constructed simple, two-room structures with stucco walls and thatched roofs. Through time and experimentation, adjusting to climate and geographical conditions and utilizing available natural resources, they began to evolve a vernacular architecture appropriate to the locale. The houses had flat or low-pitched gable roofs, entrances on the long side of the house, paired doors, *rejas* on street windows, inside shutters, side porches, loggias, street balconies, arches, outside stairs, and courtyards.

As the French, English, Dutch, and Danes initiated their colonizing efforts in the West Indies in the early 1600s, they were building on the experience of over a hundred years of Spanish colonization. The Spanish West Indian colonies boasted active ports, thriving economies, and an established agricultural base (primarily sugarcane, tobacco, and cotton). They also had strictly planned settlements with strong architectural and cultural forms and traditions.

Since the Dutch and Danes had little, if any, influence on the Louisiana colony, their contributions will not be included herein.

The French

The first efforts at colonization in the New World by the French were in Canada, a climate to which they were more accustomed than the balmy Caribbean. They founded Quebec in 1608 and Montreal in 1642. In 1648, they ventured into the West Indies and by 1665 had founded St. Barthelemy, Martinique, Guadalupe, St. Martin,

Grenada, St. Lucie, and Saint-Domingue (Haiti).

In the French West Indian settlements, like the Spanish, engineers designed the government buildings and buildings of importance. These buildings were executed in the style of the homeland—specifically, of Paris—predominantly Renaissance and neoclassical. By the time the French began to settle in the Caribbean, the Spanish, colonial, Creole farmhouse, with its broad front galleries, rear cabinets, and open loggia, were common place (Edwards 1988). The early houses of the commoners were simple, two-room rectangular structures. However, over time, the residential architecture of the French colonists began to respond to local environmental conditions and drew upon the building experiences of the earlier Spanish colonists. The evolution of a true Creole vernacular architecture had begun.

The English

The first colonial efforts of the English were, like the French in Canada, in cooler climates. On the North Atlantic coast, they settled Jamestown in 1607, Plymouth in 1620, and Charleston in 1670. Their West Indies settlements in the seventeenth century included Barbados, Nevis, Antigua, Montserrat, St. Kitts, Jamaica, and St. Vincent.

The English engineers also created buildings reflective of the styles popular in England at the time. Major buildings were strongly inspired by the classical traditions. The houses of the commoners were simple rectangular structures, not unlike those of the French; like the French settlers, the British were also inspired by the older and more established Spanish design and building techniques and joined in the evolution of a cross-cultural Creole vernacular.

The Africans

Throughout this era of colonization, Africans were brought in great numbers to the New World as slaves. While their labor was primarily directed to agricultural endeavors, they no doubt provided a vast portion of the labor required to construct the New World settlements. Doubtless, their culture influenced the development of the Creole vernacular; the extent of this influence has never been adequately documented or understood.

CREOLE VERNACULAR

The West Indies has a stormy political history. Continuous struggles, invasions, and wars resulted in frequent changes in the European "ownership" of the island colonies. West Indian port cities such as Havana and Santo Domingo became key points of entry into the New World—where goods from Europe were distributed to the surrounding Caribbean and mainland colonies—and key points of departure—where precious metals and agricultural products were collected and sent back to the European continent. These ports provided increased opportunity for cross-cultural interaction between the Spanish, French, and English. Shared experiences between these cultures resulted in a constant blending of ideas. Each culture borrowed from the others, incorporating into their own settlements and architecture the ideas and elements that had been proven successful and learning from the mistakes of those who had gone before. However, because of the independent nature of each island, distinctions between their architectural character prevailed, even among those islands colonized by the same European culture (Crain 1994). While natural resources played a major role in those distinctions, it was the climate that was the most influential force in creating continuity of the islands' architecture.

Interaction between the Spanish, French, and English fostered experimentation and the evolution of a vernacular tradition that is neither Spanish, French, nor English; it is *Creole*—a unique blending of traditions originating in Europe and evolved in the West Indies.

It is impossible to understand the cultural and architectural history of New Orleans outside of this Creole vernacular tradition. A port city itself, colonial New Orleans developed later than many of the Caribbean settlements, drawing upon their nearly two hundred years of experience. Like its source in the West Indies, the architecture of New Orleans evolved in response to climatic conditions, natural resources for building, and the traditions of a diverse blend of cultures to produce an architecture, and consequently a lifestyle, that are distinctively New Orleans.

FRENCH COLONIAL LOUISIANA 1699—1762

THE COLONIAL HISTORY OF LOUISIANA begins, for practical purposes, with the French explorations originating from Canada in the late seventeenth century. Although the Spanish had explored the Louisiana area in search of the Mississippi River as early as the fifteenth century, their first expeditions never resulted in colonial settlements.

In 1682, Robert Cavelier, Sieur de La Salle, a French Canadian fur trader, traveled south down the Mississippi from the Great Lakes to the Gulf of Mexico. Near the mouth of the Mississippi River, he set up a cross bearing the arms of France, claiming all of midcontinental America drained by the Mississippi and its tributaries for King Louis XIV and naming it Louisiane in his honor.

THE GULF COAST SETTLEMENTS

The goal of Louis XIV was to control the Mississippi Valley fur trade and provide a base of defense against Spanish and English encroachment. In 1698, he commissioned another French Canadian, Pierre Le Moyne, Sieur d'Iberville, to lead an expedition in another attempt at establishing a colony near the mouth of the Mississippi. King Louis's instructions were to go to the Mississippi River, select a good site for a town that could easily be defended, and block entry into the river from other nations. Accompanied by his younger brother, Jean Baptiste Le Moyne, Sieur de Bienville, Iberville sailed from Brest, France, on October 24, 1698. Three months later, in January of 1699, Iberville and his men reached their destination, exploring the area around present-day Biloxi, Mississippi, before venturing westward around Bay St. Louis and on to the Mississippi River. They returned to the eastern shore of Biloxi Bay, at present-day Ocean Springs, and built Fort Maurepas, thus establishing the first permanent French settlement in the province of Louisiana. They named it Biloxi, after the local Indians.

Settlers soon began arriving at the new settlement, coming from France, French Canada, and the French West Indies. Iberville, following the policies of his Canadian predecessors, immediately began forging peaceful relationships with the local Indian tribes.

In 1702, the colony was moved from Biloxi to a bluff overlooking the Mobile River, a few miles above Mobile Bay. Nine years later, it was relocated to present-day Mobile. Iberville left Bienville in charge and sailed back to France, never to return to Louisiana. He died in Havana in 1706, most likely from a bout with malaria.

Growth in the Gulf Coast settlements was slow in the early years. The 1712 census listed the population in the region from Mobile to New Orleans and up the Mississippi to Natchez at 324. Several problems inhibited growth in the region. The largest hindrance was the shallow water in Mobile Bay and the Mississippi Sound at Biloxi, which inhibited the shipment of goods from the homeland. Frequent tropical storms and occasional destructive hurricanes, sandy soil unfit

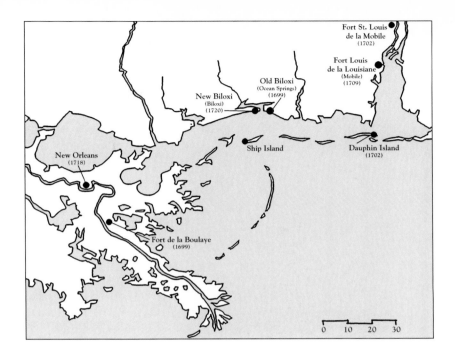

for agriculture, mosquitoes, and fever epidemics presented ongoing challenges.

Tense political conflicts in Europe distracted the French government from providing the small, troubled colony of Louisiana with needed support and supplies. Deportation of prisoners to Louisiana became a convenient means of finding settlers for the colony. Convicts had their sentences commuted and were sent to Louisiana to work for three years, after which they were given a part of the land they had cleared and cultivated.

25

THE FOUNDING OF NEW ORLEANS

While the fortified settlements at Biloxi and Mobile were important to the colonization efforts of the French, they were also ancillary to the goal of establishing a permanent city to control the Mississippi River Valley. Since the early explorations, the search for a permanent site for the capital of the Louisiana colony was ongoing. It was generally acknowledged that it should be located on the Mississippi River rather than the Gulf of Mexico. A number of sites had been explored and considered from near the mouth of the river to as far north as present-day Baton Rouge, approximately one hundred and fifty miles upstream.

As the search continued, the advantages of locating the city on the crescent of the river, near the Indian portage route to Bayou St. John and Lake Pontchartrain, were becoming increasingly acknowledged. Traveling over the portage route that led from the river, one could reach Bayou St. John and navigate his way to Lake Pontchartrain, on to Lake Bourgne and the open Gulf. This was a much shorter, quicker, and safer route to the Gulf of Mexico and the Gulf Coast settlements.

Early in 1718, three ships arrived at the Mobile colony with men, money, and supplies. Bienville, realizing an opportunity, left with about fifty men and made his way west to the chosen site on the lower Mississippi River, approximately 100 miles inland from its mouth. At a crescent-shaped bend on the east bank of the river, first explored in 1699, which by this time had become generally accepted as the best location for the capital, he commenced clearing for a new settlement.

A small section of wilderness was cleared along the riverfront and temporary housing, crude at best, was constructed. In an effort to protect the settlement from the yearly spring floods, a small levee was built along the riverbank. Bienville named the new capital Nouvelle Orleans, in honor of the Duc d'Orléans who, upon the death of Louis XIV in 1715, had become regent of France.

Arrival of the Engineers

With a site selected for the colony's capital, trained engineers were sent to prepare a plan for the new city and construct the necessary fortifications. Pierre Leblond de La Tour and his assistants, Sieurs Adrien de Pauger, Chevalier de Boispinel, and Charles Franquet de Chaville, arrived at Old Biloxi in March of 1720. Soon thereafter, the decision was made to relocate the colony to the west side of the bay, at present-day Biloxi. There they began laying out a new settlement that they called New Biloxi. Construction began on Fort Louis. A year later, they decided to move the capital to New Orleans.

Adrien de Pauger arrived in New Orleans in March 1721—his task, to execute the plan that had been developed in Biloxi under La Tour's guidance.

The Plan of the Quarter

Although Bienville had founded New Orleans some three years prior to Pauger's arrival, very little progress had been made at the site. A small area had been cleared and the direction of a few streets had been established, but only a few crude huts had been constructed.

The earliest known plan of New Orleans, designed by La Tour and Pauger, is unsigned but sent with Pauger's letter to Paris in August of 1721. Historian Sam Wilson writes: "The plan was a simple gridiron, based on the military planning principles of Louis XIV's great military engineer, the Mare'chal de Vauban, and his successor, the Marquis d'Asfeld, in whose Corps of Engineers both Leblond de La Tour and Pauger had served in Europe (Wilson 1987)."

While the plan as executed by the engineers was heavily influenced by Vauban, the origin of the grid is not French but has its roots in Hellenic Greece in the sixth and fifth centuries B.C. Driven by their instinct for orderliness, harmony, and beauty, the Greeks set out to create cities deliberately, establishing a plan to guide their growth in an orderly fashion. Their system for ordering this growth was a "gridiron" plan, with straight streets crossing at right angles and centered around a core, the agora (the equivalent of the Spanish *plaza mayor,* and the modern town square). The Greek plan, introduced into southern Italy, was spread throughout Europe by the Romans as the structure of their military camps. After a temporary eclipse during the Middle Ages, it was revived in Europe in the Renaissance of the fifteenth and sixteenth centuries.

The gridiron plan, introduced to the New World by the Spanish, became the model for colonial fortified towns and can be found in Spanish, French, and English colonial cities. In New Orleans, it was an appropriate solution to many of the problems and concerns facing the new settlement.

The first of these problems was protecting the colonists from attack by hostile Indians, the Spanish, and the English. Consequently, the size of the town was limited by the resources available to construct protective walls around the settlement. While water was abundant, supplied by the Mississippi River and the collection of rainwater in raised cisterns, the food supply was more problematic. Latter-day plantations, capable of sustaining a growing population, were not yet established. Each family was largely responsible for production of its own food, primarily in the rear yards of their residences. Lots were therefore designed large enough for houses as well as gardens, orchards, and yards for chickens and pigs.

The plan of the French Quarter, similar to those developed by the Spanish in their colonial settlements, centered around the Place d'Armes, the town commons, which served as a gathering place for the general populace and as the venue for military processions and exercises. Located on the riverfront, the Place d'Armes occupied a typical block, measuring approximately 320 feet square. The church, centrally located on the north side facing the river, was flanked by a guardhouse and prison on the left and the *Presbytère*, which was the lodging and offices of the priests, on the right. The south side was open to the river. Government buildings and houses of the aristocrats were placed in prominent locations near the Place d'Armes, while the houses of the commoners were located just beyond.

The original plan by La Tour, dated April 23, 1722, shows the Quarter divided in a grid of fifty-four square blocks. Nine months later in January 1723, the plan was expanded to sixty-six blocks, each approximately 320 feet by 320 feet. Each block was divided into

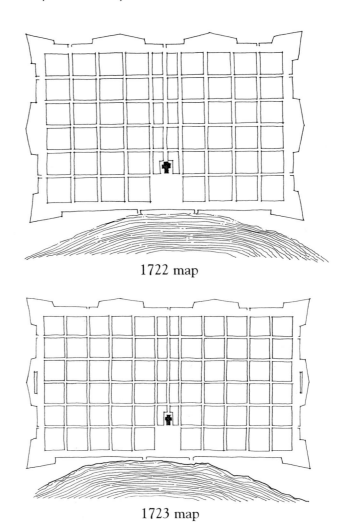

1722 map

1723 map

27

twelve lots, with five lots facing the streets parallel to the river and a key lot facing each of the perpendicular streets. The central blocks north of the church were further subdivided, placing the rear of the church on axis with each street, making it a prominent focal point from both the front and rear facades. Located directly on the banks of the river, the city proved to be very vulnerable to flooding. The seriousness of the flooding problem was not realized at the time of its founding but is well documented in records of the early years. A note on a 1719 sketch, attributed to J. M. de Beauvilliers, describes the conditions: "The islands or squares of the inhabitants are surrounded with water for three months of the year because of the overflowing of the waters of the river from the 25 March until the 24 June. In front of the town is a levee and in the rear a ditch and other drains."

Drouot de Valdeterre writes: "New Orleans is established in muddy ground brought on by the waters that overflow twice a year. . . . The waters stagnate there from two to three months and render the air very unhealthy; there are only some wooden huts absolutely beyond condition to serve if they are not repaired after each overflow." From Claude Joseph Villars Dubreuil, a royal commissioner: "The establishment of New Orleans in the beginning was awful, the river when it was high spreading over the whole ground, and in all the houses there were two feet of water, which caused general and mortal diseases."

The battle with the river—a battle which continues to this day in New Orleans—had commenced. It was not until 1790, when levee construction ensued in earnest, that the colonists began to get the flooding problem under control.

28

THE EARLY FRENCH TOWN

The natural environment posed tremendous challenges to the settlers of the Louisiana colony. Torrential rains, hurricanes, insects, flooding, scorching-hot and humid summers, and soft soils presented great obstacles to development. Although written in 1819, an entry from Benjamin Latrobe's journal describes soil conditions similar to those encountered by the new colonists.

"The Mineralogist is completely baffled in this country . . . It is a pity, as to the mere expense of building that this is a floating city, floating below the surface of the water on a bed of mud. In digging the trench for my Suction pipe, a pick could with difficulty penetrate the crust of the road, so exceedingly hard is the Clay or Mud of which after three or four days dry weather, it is compacted. But two feet six inches below the surface the blunt handle of the pick could easily be pushed down, up to the blade, and the water followed it when drawn out . . . It is very singular however that this Mass of soft stuff does not appear to permit the heavy piers that are every where built upon it, to sink gradually and constantly down. They certainly stay where they are first placed, though you may thrust a pole 20 feet into the foundation."

It was an enormous task to build a city in this kind of wilderness and with these kinds of obstacles. For the settlers, finding building solutions to these challenges came slowly and painfully, but over time, their efforts resulted in a distinctive architecture that responded to the extremities of New Orleans' climate and reflected the tenacity, strength, and creativity of the their perseverance.

The original French colonial village—the French Quarter—differed from the Spanish colonial settlements in that the houses of the commoners in the Quarter were single-story, detached dwellings, often set back from the front property lines. They were constructed on lots large enough to provide for a small garden and animal raising in the rear yard (fig.1). By contrast, Spanish colonial villages, although also one story high, were attached structures built directly on the front property line. The houses turned inward and the rear yards were private courtyards (fig. 2).

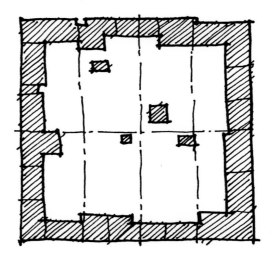

(*Fig.* 1) French-colonial block   (*Fig.* 2) Spanish-colonial block

29

THE BUILDING TRADITIONS

The early buildings in New Orleans and the surrounding Louisiana colony derived from a number of traditions. The principal formative influences were the French Canadian explorers who guided the colony in its early years; the European French, led by the engineers; and the French, West Indian Creoles. From the very earliest days of colonization, almost every ship leaving France stopped at the port of Cap François (later Cap-Haïtien) on its way to the Louisiana colony. This stopover introduced both the French Canadians and European French to the West Indian Creole building traditions and would eventually influence their traditions.

Colonial dwellings in the Louisiana colony derive their basic form and plan from two sources: the asymmetrical "Norman plan," inspired by the vernacular architecture of northwestern France, and the symmetrical "Italo-Spanish West Indian Creole house." The Norman plan, a simple rectangular core most typically comprised of a living room and a smaller bedroom, was embellished with outdoor living spaces (galleries) on at least one side, but often on all four. The Italo-Spanish plan, also a basic rectangular core, consisted of a central living room flanked on each side by smaller bedrooms, also with peripheral galleries (Edwards 1999).

The French Canadians

Aided by a tradition of exploration and settlement along the Mississippi River, the French Canadian settlers of Louisiana paved the way for much of the early development in the colony. They first constructed temporary shelters, and after stabilizing the settlement, followed with more permanent structures. The latter buildings were rectangular in shape with steeply pitched hipped roofs, similar to those found in French Quebec and Normandy at that time. The earliest construction method used by the French Canadians is called *poteaux-en-terre* (post-in-ground). Close-set vertical posts were set into the ground and extended up to form the frame of the building; the walls were held together at the top by wall plates, which supported the roof rafters.

Another method, less common in Louisiana, was called *pièce-sur-pièce*, consisting of logs laid horizontally and interlocked with dovetail notching at the corners. This method originated in ancient Europe and was carried to the New World by the French.

The European French

The early European French settlers, coming primarily from Nantes, La Rochelle, and St. Malo in northern and western France, brought many of their building techniques and traditions with them. Most of their early houses were inspired by French farmhouses.

The French military engineers, with the task of designing the essential military and government buildings (as well as many nongovernmental structures), were more influential in the development of the architecture than were the commoners. While few buildings remain from the early French colonial period, numerous drawings prepared by the French engineers have been preserved, and they clearly illustrate the character of these structures. Since these drawings were primarily structural illustrations, they do not show how the completed buildings actually looked—doors, windows, and exterior cladding are not depicted. Fortunately, there is sufficient historical documentation to piece together a more accurate description.

Strongly influenced by the neoclassical principles in vogue at the time in Paris, the engineers constructed buildings in a simplified French Renaissance style, although the building materials and labor resources at their disposal in the new colony severely limited their ability to match the achievements in France. Although they were exposed to Creole building traditions in the West Indian ports they visited, they ignored much of the observed vernacular wisdom in their early efforts. They constructed buildings with few features designed to deal with the local climate and geographic conditions, and as a result, many of their early building efforts were serious failures.

In basic form, the buildings of the engineers were similar to those of the commoners—rectangular with high-pitched hipped roofs. They were distinguished, however, by added embellishments in detailing and ornament, such as French medieval segmental arches over doors and windows. They were symmetrically designed, with a centrally located entrance. Other European French traditions included shutters, French doors, casement windows, buildings constructed low to the ground, and fireplaces.

Construction of the early buildings of the engineers was of a technique called *poteaux-sur-solle*, (posts-on-a-sill), an improvement over *poteaux-en-terre*. It consisted of the placement of vertical timbers on a heavy timber sill resting directly on the ground. In some cases a double sill was utilized, with one buried directly below grade. The exterior walls were covered with weatherboard siding. Another method was *colombage*, a half-timber construction technique common at the time in Normandy and elsewhere in western Europe where wood was available for construction. It consisted of widely spaced, vertically squared timbers with the space between filled with various materials. In Normandy this infill, called nogging, was most often broken-clay tile or cut stone; in Louisiana, *brique-entre-poteaux* (brick-between-posts) and *bousillage* (a combination of mud, lime, and a binder such as Spanish moss or horsehair) were used. The exte-

rior walls were covered with weatherboard siding or stucco to provide protection from the torrential rains that were a common occurrence in the colony.

West Indian Creoles

A constant flow of people and commerce existed between Saint-Domingue, the French jewel of the Caribbean, and the Louisiana colony from the time of its founding. While the early colonists, including the French Canadians and the European French engineers, were influenced by Creole vernacular architecture developed in the West Indies, it was the West Indian Creoles coming to Louisiana from the Caribbean, primarily Saint-Domingue, who popularized its traditions. Having had the experience of almost a century of building in the tropical climate of the islands, as well as learning from the even longer experience of the Spanish, the Creoles were much better prepared for the Louisiana environment than were the European French or the French Canadians.

The Creole vernacular architecture that the Creoles brought to Louisiana was a blending of Spanish and French influences. The typical house was a simple rectangular module consisting of three rooms arranged symmetrically (bedroom-living room-bedroom) with three openings on the front facade—a door in the center, flanked by a window on each side. Attached to this basic core, houses often had *cabinets* and *loggias*.

The most permanent building traditions brought to colonial Louisiana by the West Indian Creoles were buildings raised above the ground, galleries, two-story structures with masonry on the first floor and wood frame above, and broken pitch roofs. Houses were generally one room deep to allow for cross ventilation, with multiple French doors opening onto expansive galleries supported by slender, turned, or chamfered columns. They had high-pitched hipped roofs, broken by a shallower pitch that extended over the surrounding galleries. The roofs were covered with bark, thin boards, or wooden shingles.

Houses were generally raised two or three feet above the ground (resting on cypress stumps spaced approximately six feet apart or on solid brick foundations). This tradition evolved in response to damp soil conditions and periodic flooding.

However, the custom can also be traced to developments in the sugarcane industry in the seventeenth-century Caribbean. As the industry grew, houses for African slaves were often prefabricated and shipped to new plantation sites where they could be quickly assembled. Over time, as the fertility of the soil was depleted, the entire plantation, including the slave dwellings, was relocated. Raising the buildings facilitated the relocation process.

Houses raised a full story (eight to ten feet above the ground) were also common. Constructed along the Gulf Coast as early as the 1720s, the houses' ground levels were used for storage and workspace, and the living areas were located on the upper level. The lower floor was generally constructed of brick with a coat of plaster, and the second level of colombage with weatherboard siding. The raised house provided

33

protection from flooding, dampness, snakes and other wildlife, and also made the second-floor living space more accessible to cooling breezes in the summer. This building type, though brought to Louisiana by the Creoles, was common on farms throughout Europe.

Galleries, a major characteristic of Creole vernacular architecture, were introduced in the Louisiana colony in the early 1700s. Galleries were incorporated on one or more sides and frequently on all four. They were supported by massive columns, round or square, at the first level and by slender colonnettes, turned or chamfered, on the upper level.

While the galleries of Louisiana have their historical source in the traditions of the West Indian Creoles, according to Jay Edwards, there was a discernible African influence.

> "African slaves were imported indirectly to Hispaniola beginning in 1510, and directly (from the Guinea coast) after 1517 . . . If the pattern in Hispaniola is parallel to that of other Caribbean colonies, the newly arrived slaves were afforded considerable freedom in the design, construction, and modification of their rural houses until late in the seventeenth century.
>
> Africans . . . commonly used full length front galleries as the principal daytime living spaces in their indigenous houses. In tropical forest areas, galleries often symbolized authority and prestige and were a prominent feature of the great houses of many African chiefs and kings. Because most of the newly arriving slaves had come from these same coastal areas, the conclusion that Africans helped to introduce this tropical architectural adaption into the American environment seems inescapable, particularly in the case of the smaller country houses."

However, galleries were also used for the manor houses in Normandy, France, built in the fifteenth and sixteenth centuries. As described by Régis Faucon in *Manor Houses in Normandy*: "The upper gallery is a motif frequently found in *logis* [manor houses] built in the Pays d'Auge [Normandy] between the late 15th and mid 16th centuries. Accessed from the staircase turret, mostly open, and covered by a roof supported by a row of narrow posts, the gallery could either project fully or rest on projecting beams over the timber portico situated on the ground floor."

The use of galleries greatly influenced the evolution of vernacular roof forms. As galleries were added to the basic rectangular modules, roof forms evolved from a simple lean-to attachment to a double-pitched roof, and eventually, to the single-pitched "umbrella roof," which covered the main body of the house as well as the galleries. (Edwards 1988)

While French Creole vernacular architecture can be found in French settlements throughout the West Indies, it was in the great sugar colonies of Saint-Domingue, Cayenne (French Guiana), and Louisiana that the French constructed houses with all of the Creole features as described above (Edwards 1994).

THE COLONY GROWS

After temporary shelters were constructed and the settlement stabilized, more permanent structures had to be built. The first buildings of importance in the French Quarter, constructed by the engineers, were the director's house (*fig.* 3 and opposite page)—designed by La Tour in 1722—carpenters' barracks (*fig.* 4), and the hospital (*fig.* 5). Rectangular structures of heavy timber framing, they were constructed on timber sills laid directly on the ground. The exterior walls were covered with wide boards and roofed with wooden shingles or strips of bark. The director's house, located on the corner of Decatur and Toulouse Streets, was designed as the administrative building for the directors of the Company of the Indies. It was described by Pauger as "the most beautiful house that has yet been seen in the colonies, and an example to the settlers in building their own houses (Wilson 1987)."

(*Fig.* 4)

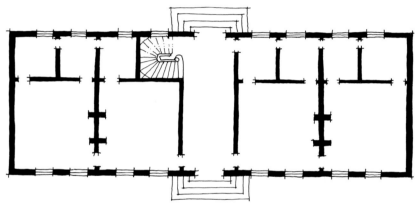

(*Fig.* 3)

(*Fig.* 5)

Powder Magazine

36

Lloyd Vogt

Upon La Tour's death in 1723, Adrien de Pauger was appointed chief engineer. He immediately began work on a new warehouse, powder magazine, and wing for the hospital, and in 1724, he designed the parish church (*fig.* 6) on the same site where the St. Louis Cathedral is located today. In 1726, Pauger died and upon his request was buried beneath the church, which was under construction at the time. Ignace François Broutin, a military captain who had come to the colony with La Tour in 1720, assumed the role of chief engineer and oversaw the completion of the church.

As the colony grew, construction problems began to appear. The early colonial wooden structures built on ground sills experienced rapid decay in the humid climate and continual subsidence in the soft soils, prompting a search for more appropriate construction methods.

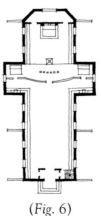

(*Fig.* 6)

Under the direction of Pierre Baron, a technique of half-timber construction with the timbers and brickwork left exposed was introduced. Although common in France at the time, in the French Quarter, because of the porous nature of the local brick and the subtropical rains, exposed brick construction resulted in rapid deterioration—all the buildings so constructed had to be rebuilt within a few years.

In 1726 the first brickyard was established on Bayou St. John. In a letter dated May 6, 1727, Broutin asked that more brick masons be sent to the colony "in order to be able to do all the proposed buildings in brick and on piles so that they may be works to remain and endure (McDermott-Wilson 1969)." In 1731, Baron, presiding as chief engineer, designed a prison beside the parish church, facing the Place d'Armes, the site now occupied by the Cabildo. It was the first all-brick structure recorded in New Orleans.

The guardhouse and prison (proposed to be constructed at the Basile located at the mouth of the Mississippi River from drawings signed by the military engineer Bernard de Deverges and dated February 28, 1734) illustrates the influence of the West Indian vernacular tradition on the young colony with the incorporation of galleries (*fig.* 7). Its appearance contrasts with the buildings of the French engineers.

The Doctor's House (*fig.* 8), designed by Broutin in 1735, was a small two-story house with a steeply pitched, hipped roof and dormers. Fenestrations were on the front and rear facades, with the side walls supporting fireplaces and chimneys. Windows had segmental arch tops and the entrance incorporated a fanlight transom above the door. The house was ornamented with quoins and belt courses, and stucco bands accentuated the openings. The overall appearance borrowed much of its inspiration from Paris, France. Research indicates that the house was never constructed; however, it is a good example of the design sensibilities of the early colonial period.

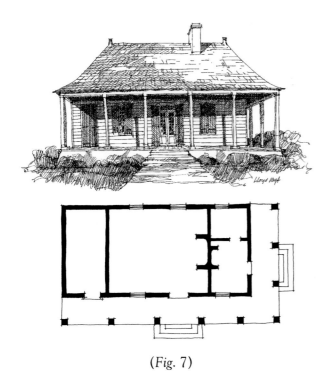

(*Fig.* 7)

(*Fig.* 8)

Building upon experience, the engineers continued to experiment with different construction techniques. Their buildings rotted, sunk into the soil, were devoured by termites, and blown down by hurricanes. Eventually, a combination of two construction methods, brick on the first level and *colombage* on the second, proved to be a viable solution and became the typical method of construction from about the mid-1700s to the late 1700s.

With an established capital at New Orleans, there was a slow but steady influx of immigrants to the colony. Almost all of the Louisiana settlements were located on waterways, and most settlers traveled to nearby villages in some kind of boat—most often a pirogue, a small flat-bottomed boat resembling a canoe. The Mississippi River, with its tributaries, was Louisiana's great means of commerce, and trade with France and the French and Spanish West Indies, its lifeblood.

In the 1720s, the Company of the Indies brought several thousand German and Swiss farmers into the colony to satisfy the food shortage. They settled approximately forty miles upriver from New Orleans, in what is now Des Allemands and proved to be an important factor in saving the colony from starvation during its early years.

In order to meet the need for labor to construct the new towns and support the agricultural economy, African slaves were imported to the colony. Coming first from the West Indies, then directly from Africa, almost all the slaves brought to Louisiana under French rule, approximately 5,700, arrived between 1718 and 1731. The majority came from a single region of Africa, the Senegal River Basin, bringing with them an already formed Bambara culture. By the 1730s, the slave population was approximately twice that of the whites. Aided by the increased labor force, larger farms began to evolve. As the colony grew, commerce increased; from the Louisiana ports of New Orleans, Biloxi, and Mobile skins and hides, indigo, tobacco, myrtle wax, bear's oil, pitching tar, and lumber were shipped. From the French ports of La Rochelle, Brest, and Bordeaux, and from the West Indian ports of Havana, Port-au-Prince, Santo Domingo, and Cap-Haitien came food, flowers, wine, clothing, spices, utensils, and other goods.

In 1731, the Company of the Indies, failing to make an economic success of the Louisiana venture, ceded control of the colony back to the Crown and ceased the shipment of supplies. The planters, realizing the advantages of a stable slave society but now, in many instances, no longer able to care for and feed their slaves, no longer required them to work on Sundays and religious holidays. On these days, they were allowed to leave the plantations and take on jobs for pay. They also began to work their own gardens and to hunt, fish, and trap or gather fruit, nuts, and firewood, which they would take into town to sell. Soon, they were given Saturday afternoons off and assigned plots of land on which to grow their own food, as well as barns and bins in which to store it. Eventually, many of the slaves became self-supporting, participating in the New Orleans market economy (Hirsch 1992). By the end of the French period, slaves were holding Sunday market on the edge of the Quarter at the end of Orleans Street, an area that became known as Congo Square.

Under a series of French colonial governors guided by Bienville, the colony slowly grew. The Gonichon plan of New Orleans, drawn in 1731, depicts a city of buildings with high hip roofs, some with galleries, and most set from ten to fifteen feet from the front property line. They were detached structures, and in the rear yards were gardens, orchards, arbors, and service buildings such as kitchens, privies, storehouses, stables, and slave quarters.

The increasing activity added to the boisterous character of the colonists. When the Marquis de Vaudreuil, the son of a former governor of Canada, came to town in 1743, he was horrified, as his earlier predecessor Governor Cadillac had been, at the rowdiness of the colony's population. Like Cadillac, he resolved to civilize the people (Hirsch 1992).

The fall of French Quebec to the English in 1759 left the Mississippi Valley vulnerable to British invasion. The fortified protection of New Orleans was greatly lacking, consisting of only forts at Bayou St. John and Lake Pontchartrain and partial palisades on the border of the city. This new threat prompted the French courts to immediately upgrade the fortification by constructing five redoubts connected by ramparts with a surrounding ditch (Parkerson 1991).

Although the colony was experiencing growth (during the 1750s nearly a hundred houses were constructed in the Quarter), it continued to fail as an economic venture, so France began directing more and more support and resources to saving its West Indian colonies, eventually ignoring the costly and unsuccessful Louisiana colony. Despite the lack of French support, a population of approximately 3,000—made up of French, French Canadians, West Indians, Creoles, Germans, Swiss, African and mulatto slaves, and free men of color—continued to battle the elements. Through Benjamin Latrobe's relation of the conditions in 1819, his description of the relentless pest, the mosquito, would have been similar to that encountered by the colonists during this period.

"But the pest inseparable from the locality of New Orleans which no human effort can extirpate, are the Muskitoes, the *Marangouins*. A few are found, every warm day throughout the Year, but from June to the Middle of October or beginning of November, their swarms are incredible. The Muskitoes are so important a body of enemies, that they furnish a considerable part of the conversation of every day, and of every body; they regulate many family arrangements, they prescribe the employment and distribution of time, and most essentially affect the comfort and enjoyment of every individual in the country.

As soon as the sun sets, the Muskitoes appear in Clouds, and fill every room in the house, as well as the open Air. Their noise is so loud, as to startle a stranger to its daily recurrence. It fills the air, and there is a character of occasionally depression and elevation in it, like that of a concert of frogs in a Marsh. There may also be distinguished, I think, four or five leading voices that are occasionally swelled and intermitted; in fact the whole music has the effect of being performed by unanimous concert. This Noise and the activity of these pestiferous animals lasts about an hour, when it abates and almost ceases. The buzzing may however be heard through' the whole night, until daybreak, when the general Outcry again begins, more loudly, I think, than in the evening, and continued till the Sun has risen, when it ceases, and no more is heard, and little felt, till the approach of the night.

The numbers, the minuteness, and the activity of these enemies to repose, render any warfare against them that is not merely defensive impossible. But a defensive war is very practicable and may be in a great measure successful. The business of the greatest importance is to secure yourself against their attacks during sleep. The common Muskitoe bar effects this most completely. It consists of Curtains reaching from the Tester nearly to the floor, which surround the bed in one piece, connected by a cover or top piece, so that the Muskitoe bar is a kind of box without a bottom. The best kind of Muskitoe bar, is furnished all round the top with rings. The rings slide as in a common set of curtains upon light Iron rods on each side of the bed . . . and there is an indescribably pleasant sense of serenity in hearing their clamor on the outside without the possibility of being annoyed by them. The bars are made either of coarse open canvass, French lino (which are the best), Silk, open and figured Gauze (which are the most handsome), and most frequently of check Muslin."

While the Louisiana colony had never been of great interest to French commerce because it had neither sugar nor coffee and because its export products could be found in greater quantities in the other colonies, it was, however, of great interest to Saint-Domingue. Having quickly depleted their limited supply of timber while experiencing growth in both cities and plantations, the island was badly in need of wood for construction and casks, and firewood for the furnaces of its sugar mills. The forests of the Louisiana colony, with excellent timber supplies, satisfied these needs. As described by Le Page du Pratz, a director of the Company of the Indies plantation at New Orleans in the early 1700s: "From Louisiana, they took to the islands squared cypress beams suitable for building. Houses, completely marked and cut, ready to assemble upon arrival at their destination, were often transported; brick; essentes (flat wood shingles) used to cover homes and barns." It appears that an evolving Creole vernacular architecture was flowing from New Orleans to the Caribbean, as well as from the Caribbean to New Orleans.

By 1760, as the French regime was coming to an end, much of the Quarter was still unimproved. Only the first four streets from the river were fully developed and the large majority of the houses were simple, wooden, one-story structures—the better houses were two stories with galleries. Most of the important buildings constructed by the French had disappeared. It had been a period of tremendous hardship encountered with great perseverance—the colonists demonstrating great ingenuity in merely surviving. France had tried, but had never been able, to make Louisiana a profitable venture.

URSULINE CONVENT

1114 Chartres Street
1745-1750
National Historic Landmark

Arriving from Rouen, France in 1727, the Ursuline nuns came to New Orleans to run a hospital, orphanage, and school and were a very affluent and influential force in the city. The original convent was designed by Ignace François Broutin in 1727 and in his absence modified by Pierre Baron. The building took seven years to construct due to various delays. During its construction, the exterior walls had not been properly protected from the climate, and by the time the nuns moved into the building in 1734, it was already beginning to rot badly. In 1745 Broutin prepared a design for a new convent to replace the old one, incorporating parts of the old building into the plan. This building is the convent that we see today. Broutin died before its completion and the construction was overseen by his successor, Bernard de Deverges. The convent was completed in 1750 by builder Claude Joseph Villars Dubreuil.

The Ursulines occupied the convent until 1824. Since that time, it has been used as a bishopric, schoolhouse, state capital, and seminary. The building is now being used as the archives of the archdiocese.

The convent is surrounded by a high, masonry wall forming a front courtyard with a large formally planted garden. The courtyard is entered from a central gateway on axis with the building's entrance, recalling the seventeenth-century *hotels* of Paris. The building is designed in a simple elegant Louis IV style, reflective of the architectural traditions common in Paris at the time. In 1846, J. N. B. dePouilly designed the adjacent church, Notre Dame des Victoires, to complement the convent.

The Ursuline Convent is the oldest surviving building in New Orleans, as well as in the Mississippi Valley.

Lloyd Vogt

MADAME JOHN'S LEGACY

The Manuel Lanzos House
628-632 Dumaine Street
Circa 1788
National Historic Landmark

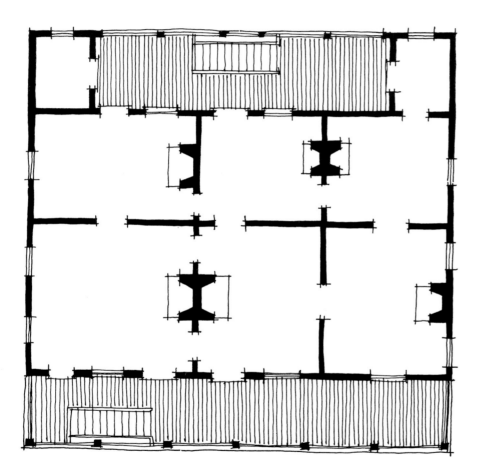

Although Madame John's was constructed after the fire of 1788, it is more appropriately included in the pre-fire era, since it was basically a reconstruction of a house type common during that time. Shortly after the fire, its owner, Don Manuel de Lanzos, a Spanish officer, contracted with Robert Jones, an American builder who had recently come to New Orleans from the new United States, to construct a house very similar to the one that had burned.

Madame John's Legacy, which derives its name from a reference in George W. Cable's story "Tite Poulette", is a very important example of colonial architecture in New Orleans. The original site extended to the corner of Royal and Dumaine Streets and was granted to the first owner shortly after the founding of the city in 1718. A map of the city drawn in 1731 indicates a building very similar in size to the present building, with the exception of the porches.

In 1777, the house was sold to Renato Beluche who, as Rene Beluche, has become associated with Lafayette the Pirate and the battle of New Orleans. Beluche sold the property the following year. Although there is speculation that the house escaped the fire that destroyed much of the Quarter in 1788, current research indicates that the building most likely burned and was rebuilt in a manner very similar to the house lost in fire.

The house is one of the few remaining examples of a type common in the Quarter in the French colonial period. The main living area of half-timber construction is raised above a first-floor storage-work area constructed of brick. A gallery spans the front of the house at the second level. The house was donated to the Louisiana State Museum by Mrs. I. I. Lemann, assuring the preservation of this extremely important landmark.

Lloyd Vogt

DUROCHE CASTILLON HOUSE

Jean Lafitte's Blacksmith Shop
941 Bourbon Street
Circa 1795
National Historic Landmark

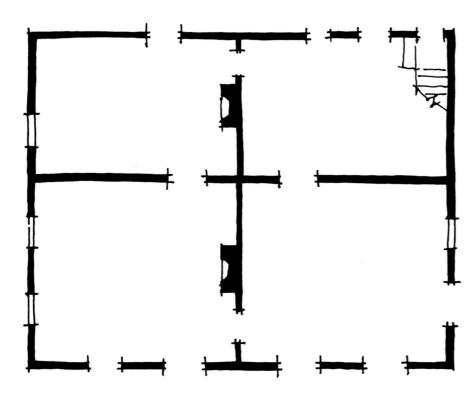

Most likely constructed around 1795, the Duroche Castillon House, romantically referred to in New Orleans as Lafitte's Blacksmith Shop, is one of the few surviving examples of a Norman cottage in the Quarter. Streets in the early French and Spanish colonial town were lined with small free-standing cottages built right up to the street with secluded gardens behind, similar to the Duroche Castillon House. Most of these houses burned during the great fires of 1788 and 1794. Those that survived were demolished and replaced.

Simon Duroche, a castellan for whom this house is named, married Margerite Robert, whose father owned property but later gave it to the couple in 1781. Duroche's widow held onto the house for over seventy years. At the time of her death in 1833, she was living in Faubourg Marigny and the house was left to the tenants. It was at this time that the infamous Lafitte brothers, pirates Jean and Pierre, allegedly occupied the house.

The plan of the house is basically square, divided into four rooms with double fireplaces between the two front and two rear rooms. The house is constructed of *colombage* and *brique-entre-poteaux*. The timbers are hand hewn and the marks are still in evidence. The building has been modified somewhat through time; it has lost its overhanging roof and dormers have been added. The exterior stucco has been removed in various locations to expose some of the brick-between-post construction.

The legend of the Lafittes operating a blacksmith shop out of the house as a cover for their smuggling activities was established by George Washington Cable in his "Pirates of Barataria"; however, there are no records to substantiate this claim.

Lloyd Vogt

THE SPANISH DOMINION 1762 (1766)—1800 (1803)

IN 1762, BY THE SECRET treaty of Fontainbleau, France ceded the Isle of Orleans, along with all of Louisiana west of the Mississippi River, to Spain, but it was not until 1764 that the French governor informed the people of Louisiana that it was now a Spanish colony. A drawing of New Orleans, as seen from the opposite side of the Mississippi River in 1765 (possibly by Capt. Philip Pittman), illustrated the distinctive character of the city at the time of the Spanish takeover; almost every building had a gallery of some kind.

At the time of the takeover, the Spanish had numerous established colonies in the West Indies, Mexico, and Central and South America, but only two settlements in North America: St. Augustine and Pensacola (Florida), neither of which had been very prosperous. Understanding the influence of the Spanish culture on the French Quarter can best be accomplished by analyzing the planning and building traditions of the Spanish colonials in their West Indian settlements, such as Havana, San Juan, and Santo Domingo. Guided by the *Laws of the Indies*, the Spanish had colonial towns with plans very similar to that of the French Quarter, a central plaza within a grid.

Havana was the most prominent Spanish colonial city in the Caribbean and Mexico City was the center of the Mexican-South American colony. Vera Cruz, on the Gulf Coast of Mexico, was the major port from which Mexican treasures were shipped, while Cartagena (Columbia) was the major port for the South American colonies. Convoys from these two ports typically stopped in Havana before proceeding to Spain.

On March 15, 1766, four years after the French colony had been ceded to the Spanish, the first Spanish governor, the respected scientist Antonio de Ulloa, arrived in New Orleans. Along with an entourage of officials and troops, he ushered in the Spanish colonial era.

Upon arrival, the Spanish received a cold reception from the locals. The French soldiers, anxious to return home, refused to join the Spanish ranks. Realizing the hostile attitude of the residents, with only ninety Spanish soldiers, Ulloa thought it unwise to attempt to take formal possession of the colony. During the following two years, funded by the Spanish government, and with the assistance of the acting French governor, Charles Phillipe Aubry, Ulloa served as an effective administrator. Meanwhile, in Havana, the Spanish were forming the Fixed Louisiana Infantry Battalion in preparation for the official takeover.

Ulloa's thirty months of administration were filled with difficulties, mostly from his rift with the French Superior Council. A body formed in 1725, the council represented the local, wealthy merchants and planters and had dominated, without controls, local trade practices. Ulloa did not think highly of the group, and he bypassed them, preferring to work with the French royal officials.

In 1767, upon Ulloa's recommendation, the Spanish government issued instructions to abolish the council as soon as the formal transfer of authority had taken place. However, Ulloa, instead of abolishing the council, opted to create a new assembly composed of three Spaniards and four Frenchmen. The new tribe gained control with much resentment from the shunned council. The conflict worsened and public opinion among the French in the community was mixed.

In 1768, the Spanish government began the process to formally take control of the colony. An earlier agreement allowing the French to trade with the French West Indian colonies and French ships to freely use the port was rescinded, restricting trade to only Spanish ports and Spanish ships. The Superior Council rebelled and ordered the expulsion of all Spaniards from the colony, except for three treasury officials who they held hostage in order to redeem the paper money and bonds in circulation. Attempting to add legitimacy to their actions, the rebels offered the position of leadership to acting

French governor Aubry; however, he was not sympathetic to their cause. He refused the position.

In April 1769, Carlos III of Spain instructed Lt. Gen. Alejandro O'Reilly to go to Havana, prepare the troops, and proceed to New Orleans to put down the rebellion. O'Reilly, an Irish-born soldier, was a highly regarded and experienced commander who had served as the Spanish army's inspector general and had participated in numerous European military campaigns. Upon his arrival in Havana, he assumed command of two thousand troops and set sail for New Orleans.

The revolt proved unsuccessful, as both France and England rejected the rebels' request for assistance. An attempt to create a separate republic gained little support, and as word of the Spanish troops in route became known, there was little interest in fighting against such overwhelming odds. The leaders of the revolt decided it was best to plead innocent and ask for clemency. The Spanish fleet arrived in New Orleans on August 17, and among cannon fire and military pageantry, O'Reilly's soldiers disembarked and assembled in the Plaza de Armas (renamed by the Spanish). In a formal ceremony, Aubry surrendered the colony to the Spanish.

Twelve individuals considered to be the leaders of the revolt were arrested and a general pardon was issued to the rest of the colonists. After two months of investigation, charges of treason, sedition, writing inflammatory documents, and leading hostile troops with the intent of overthrowing Spanish authority were levied. A trial followed and five men were condemned to death, one had already died in prison, and six others got prison terms, and the very next day, the condemned were executed by a firing squad in the courtyard of the military barracks. The other six were sent to Havana to serve their time; after only one year, they were pardoned, with the stipulation that they were never to return to Louisiana.

After taking control of the colony, O'Reilly's next task was to choose the form of government for Louisiana. He created a government patterned after those in the other Spanish colonies, formally establishing a *cabildo* in August of 1769. With New Orleans securely under Spanish control, O'Reilly left the city the next year.

The transition from French to Spanish control was not easy for the Louisiana colonists, who thought of themselves as Frenchmen and loyal subjects of King Louis XV. Early Spanish governors wisely defused the hostility by leaving the French and French Creoles in positions of authority in government and by encouraging social interaction and intermarriage between the French and the Spanish. The first years of Spanish rule in the colony were basically administrative, without considerable cultural, social, or architectural contributions. Largely due to the charisma and integrity of the early governors, the French colonists accepted the new government as well as the Spanish colonists.

The Spanish found many new settlers who established farms and plantations, making the colony self-supporting. One of the most important immigrations of Louisiana's colonial history—the settling of the Acadians on the "Acadian Coast" along the Mississippi, from Baton Rouge to New Orleans—had begun as early as 1744, but the great influx of Acadian refugees and the establishment of successful Acadian towns and settlements occurred after 1765. During the 1770s, there was also a wave of immigrants from the Canary Islands; in the 1780s, several hundred Pennsylvanians came.

The Cabildo—the Spanish, city government building—was constructed in 1769 next to the parish church, on the former site of Baron's prison of 1730. It was a one-story structure of brick-between-post construction with a front gallery supported by chamfered-wood columns.

At the time of the census of 1785, 5,000 people—approximately one-fourth whites, one-fourth free persons of color, and one-half slaves—lived in the city. The old cemetery, originally located directly outside of the city boundaries (which would now be at St. Peter and Burgundy Streets), was closed and a new one, which can still be visited, St. Louis Cemetery Number One, opened on the northern edge of the Quarter on Basin Street. Its architecture is one of tombs-above-grade and has become one of the identifying characteristics of the city.

THE GREAT FIRES: 1788 & 1794

On Good Friday, March 21, 1788, a candle burning on an altar in a house at 617 Chartres Street started a fire that destroyed more than 800 buildings (nearly eighty percent of the city), which at the time consisted primarily of small, detached, wooden buildings roofed with wood shingles, which undoubtedly fueled the conflagration.

In addition to most of the houses, destroyed were the Church of St. Louis, the Cabildo, the Corps de Garde, and the jail. Governor Miro described the fire in his correspondence to the Spanish court.

"On the 21st of March, 1788, being Good Friday, at half past one in the afternoon, a fire broke out in New Orleans, in the house of the Military Treasurer . . . and reduced to ashes eight hundred and fifty-six edifices, among which were the stores of all the merchants, and the dwellings of the principal inhabitants, the Cathedral, the Convent of the Capuchins, with greater portion of their books, the Townhall, the watch-house, and the arsenal with all its contents . . . Almost the whole of the population of the smoldering town was ruined and deprived even of shelter during the whole of the following night."

In response, to provide temporary shelter for the homeless, Governor Miro ordered that scores of canvas, army tents be set up in Plaza de Armas (Jackson Square) and on the riverfront levee. He sent ships in search of food, clothing, and supplies; however, relief efforts were inadequate for the massive devastation. Many of the homeless left the city to find shelter in the surrounding rural areas—many never returned. Those who remained met the crisis with resolve. A community of shacks strung out along the levee housed those with limited financial resources, while those more able commenced with the rebuilding of the Quarter. Yet, in spite of the overwhelming destruction that had been experienced, rebuilding continued very much as before—small wooden buildings roofed with wooden shingles. The colonists had learned little from the catastrophe and new construction was not executed with much forethought. By 1791, much of the Quarter had been rebuilt; however, the new buildings only created the conditions for yet another devastating fire.

The Second Fire: 1794

On December 8, 1794, a second great fire started on Royal Street, and once again, the Quarter was ravaged. This time over 200 buildings, including warehouses, stores, barracks, and government structures, were destroyed and extensive looting occurred, aggravating the devastation. Once again, the Plaza de Armas and the levee became camping grounds for the homeless. The second fire prompted Spanish governor Carondelet to enforce more stringent building regulations for fire prevention, and as a result, the construction that followed was more substantial and less prone to fire damage.

We can only surmise what the Quarter would be like today had the two great fires not occurred. It most likely would have grown and evolved similar to its sister city in the French colony of Saint-Domingue, Cap François (present-day Cap-Haïtien). Very similar in appearance to New Orleans in the eighteenth century, Cap François has evolved through the years with the peripheries of the city's blocks gradually being filled in with houses, shops, and other structures, while the interiors of the blocks remained more open, used for gardens and other amenities. While we can only speculate, we know that it would be quite different.

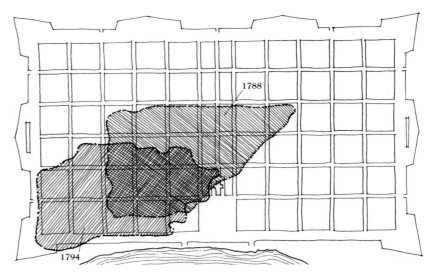

THE NEW CITY EMERGES

As a result of the two major fires, over one thousand buildings in the Quarter were lost. The buildings constructed afterwards—many of which survive today—were constructed under stringent building regulations enforced by the Spanish government, giving the Quarter much of its present-day character. Thus, New Orleans began its transformation from a struggling colonial town to a forceful New World city.

Solid, masonry, fireproof construction became the norm, detached houses with rear gardens were no longer permitted, and the Quarter soon took on a more urban character as two- and three-story attached townhouses were constructed. Roofs were required to be covered with tile in lieu of wooden shingles, and walls constructed of brick-between-posts were required to have at least an inch of protective cement plaster. Additional precautions required that all two-story houses be constructed of brick or of timber frames filled with brick between the upright posts and the timbers to be covered with cement at least one inch thick. Flat roofs were to be tiled or bricked. Small one-story wooden houses were still permitted but they were limited to thirty feet in depth, including galleries. A law adopted on October 9, 1795 mandated that all houses "must precisely have their front facing the street, and no one is allowed to build them with the rear or sides to the street except those persons whose lots have not a frontage of thirty feet."

The fires had devoured nearly all of the official public buildings, and the Spanish government had very few resources to rebuild these civic buildings. Realizing the severity of the situation, a very wealthy Spanish resident, Don Andrés Almonester y Roxas, became a major patron of the city, contributing large sums of money to the rebuilding efforts. He financed the construction of the parish church, schoolhouse, hospital, Cabildo, and Capuchin convent.

The Spanish shared a number of building characteristics with the French: paired doors (commonly referred to as French doors), casement windows, and wrought iron. Characteristics common to the Spanish but not to the French include flat roofs, projecting balconies with shed roofs, Spanish tile, stained-glass transoms (hovace), and stucco surrounds around doors and windows. Another feature common in Spanish buildings was the use of the arch and arcades, and although arches were common in major buildings in France at the time, the arch was not common in the Quarter during the French colonial era—openings almost always had segmental arches or were flat-topped.

Influenced by the traditions of southern Spain, buildings with flat roofs and flat tiles began to be constructed. Dr. John Sibley, a visitor from Natchitoches, describes the Quarter in 1802: "The greatest number of the houses, particularly those newly built are flat roofed. . . . A balustrade round ornamented with urns, balls, etc. The tops of the houses are as their back yards and the women wash, iron, sit to work and the men walk on them and of from the top of one house to the tip of another and visit their neighbors without having anything to do with the streets below. Many have shrubs and flowers growing on their houses."

From after the second fire of 1794 to the early part of the 1800s, the urban character of the Quarter evolved, initiated by the introduction of the attached townhouse. Two-, three-, and four-story buildings, with courtyards and outbuildings in the rear, became common in the heart of the Quarter between the river and Bourbon Street, while one-story Creole cottages populated the fringes. Since buildings were once again being constructed low to the ground, we can assume that the levee was by now sufficient to prevent the yearly spring flooding.

THE COURTYARD

Before describing the house types common during this period, a discussion of courtyards is helpful, since they play such an important role in defining the character and ambience of the Quarter. Whether the courtyards in the French Quarter are of French or Spanish origin is a question often raised. As discussed earlier, such cultural origins are often blurred and difficult to define, as they are often the result of cultural interaction and borrowing of ideas over an extended period of time. To understand and appreciate the courtyards of the Quarter, a historical perspective is essential.

Courtyards have a very ancient tradition, having appeared among the earliest human settlements. Examples excavated at Kahun, Egypt are believed to be 5,000 years old and examples in the Caldean city of Ur date from before 2,000 B.C. Thus the origin of the courtyard house is generally attributed to the Arab culture. More examples can be found throughout the Middle East, from where the popularity of the concept spread to Morocco, India, Jaipur, and Russia.

Courtyards were even common in ancient Greece. The typical Greek house (*fig.* 9) was built around one or more courtyards. The Romans adopted the idea from their Etruscan neighbors to the north, and when introduced to the building traditions of the Greeks living in southern Italy, combined the atrium (Etruscan) with the peristyle (Greek) for their houses (*fig.* 10). A look at Pompeii in 79 A.D. gives us a view of the Roman tradition. The Romans spread the idea throughout Europe as they expanded their empire from the first century B.C. to the fourth century A.D.

By the fourteenth century, as the medieval era drew to a close and the Renaissance emerged, Europe began to experience a tremendous growth in its urban centers. Population increases, within the confines of fortress walls still necessary for protection, created the need for a denser urban setting. As a result, cities such as Paris, London, Florence, and Barcelona responded by building upward with attached structures of multiple stories housing shops at the first level and dwellings above. Within these dense building conditions, the courtyard became a common urban form, providing calm and privacy from the noisy

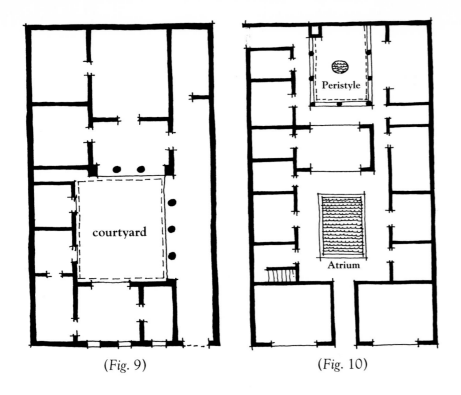

courtyard

(Fig. 9)

Peristyle

Atrium

(Fig. 10)

from the earliest years of colonization, the Spanish constructed houses with courtyards.

In France, the energy of the emerging Renaissance centered around Paris, where a renewed interest in the city brought about a conscious effort for improvement. Breaking from the medieval mode of organic growth, in 1605 the Parisians constructed Place des Vosges (Place Royale), a complex of attached townhouses with retail at the first floor, set behind an arcade. Many of these buildings had wings projecting into rear courtyards and gardens separated by high walls.

In 1623, in a pioneering book, *Manière de bien bastir pour toutes sortes de personnes*, Parisian architect Pierre Le Muet, provided guidelines for builders and patrons desiring to build a new house. He provided drawings for thirteen houses of different sizes, all with courtyards and many very similar to the Creole townhouses of the Quarter.

streets, for the palaces of the wealthy, as well as light and air circulation into the interior of densely populated urban blocks—in many cases little more than narrow shafts multiple stories high.

In Spain, the Romans had introduced the concept of the courtyard during their colonial expansion, in the first century B.C. The concept was reinforced by the Moors in Andalusia during their domination from the eighth to fifteenth century, for not only was it suited to the climate of southern Spain, but also appropriate for the Moorish value system in which proper women were sequestered and sheltered from public life, as was stated earlier, part of the Arab tradition. Its common use in Spain at the time, coupled with the similarity of the West Indian and Latin America climate to southern Spain, made it an appropriate model for Spanish settlements in the New World, and

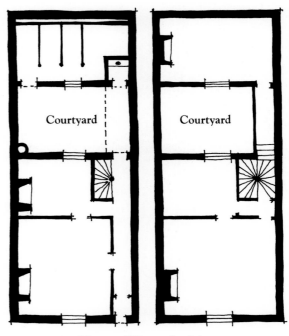

Courtyard

Courtyard

Plans of Pierre Le Muet

55

A view of the Ille de la Cite in Paris in 1754 (*fig.* 11) shows a community of townhouses with courtyards accessed by porte cochères. In plan, Paris is indistinguishable from Spanish colonial San Juan of the same period (*figs.* 12 and 13). By the late 1700s, at about the time the Quarter was about to experience its post-fire construction and the first appearance of townhouses with courtyards, the rage in Paris was the classically inspired, symmetrical building with central porte cochères and rear courtyards.

In New Orleans, the concept of the courtyard was present from its very founding. Since the pressures of land were not severe, what developed were small houses with gardens in the rear, sized to accommodate a small house at the street line with enough room in the rear for a garden, farm animals, and numerous ancillary storage and utility structures. Fences from five to eight feet in height were constructed around the property to keep farm animals in and undesirable animals out, completely enclosing the rear yard, and in effect, creating rear courtyards.

Since courtyards take many forms, a clear definition is necessary for discussion purposes. It seems that for an exterior space to be considered a courtyard, it must be enclosed on all sides and provide a certain degree of privacy. While not including the entire range of variants, the majority of courtyard houses throughout history can be classified into seven basic configurations: I, L, C, U, O, 8, and Organic (*fig.* 14). They can further be grouped into two types, utilitarian and social. The French Quarter has within its boundaries all but type "8," which, incidentally, is a typical Spanish type in Spain and the Spanish colonies.

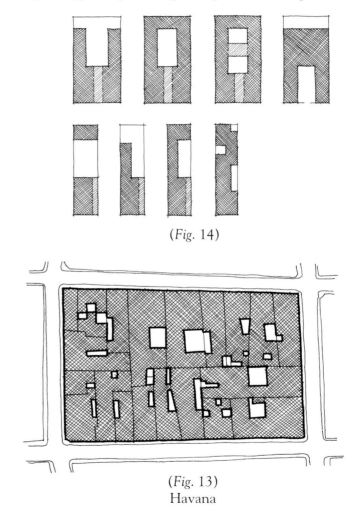

(*Fig.* 14)

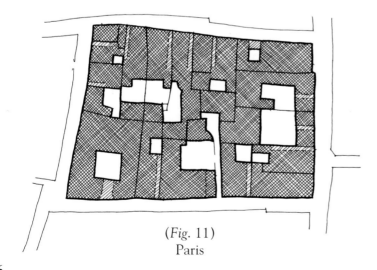

(*Fig.* 11)
Paris

(*Fig.* 13)
Havana

56

The "utilitarian" courtyard is one whose purpose is solely to allow light and air into dense multistory buildings and is not constructed for use as human habitation, while "social" courtyards are spaces that, while also allowing light and air, provide social (living and working) space at the ground level. The Quarter is comprised primarily of "social" courtyards (*fig.* 15).

In order to codify the courtyard types in the Quarter, they are generally grouped into three main types: Creole cottages with rear outbuildings, Creole townhouses (pedestrian and porte cochère), and Creole townhouses with central porte cochères.

The New Orleans Creole townhouse differs from the Spanish West Indian model in that it is comprised of two basic modules—the main structure (*corps de logis*) and an extended wing (*garçonnière*) connected by a stairwell with a winder stair, whereas the Spanish house is entirely variable, expanding room by room, depending on the wealth and needs of the owner and not adhering to any one model. Jay Edwards explains the differences: "A comparison of the patio houses of the Zona Colonial in Santo Domingo (fig 16) with those of the Vieux Carré of New Orleans (fig 17) offers a striking impression of similarity not shared by other American cities east of

San Antonio and Santa Fe. Yet, although they appear to be much alike, this appearance is an illusion if it is taken to imply a direct historical relationship." He continues, explaining that the forms of the houses differ significantly. The common "L-shaped" porte cochère townhouses of the Quarter are uncommon in Havana, Santo Domingo, or old San Juan. In the Spanish cities, the entrances to the courtyard (zaguán) are generally to narrow for a carriage, and the common shed-roofed garçonnière, extending into the rear courtyards of the porte cochère houses of the Quarter, is uncommon in Spanish cities. While the Quarter porte cochère houses seem to be modeled after a prototype, the Spanish house is variable, resulting from evolutionary patterns of expansion.

In essence, the courtyard house was a logical prototype for new construction in the Quarter after the fires, solving the two most basic problems facing the colonists: a need for increased density, as the result of a growing population, and a method of dealing with the tropical climate. By design, courtyards have a cooling effect in hot humid climates, creating shade and circulating air currents.

With an increased population and an agricultural base in the surrounding area sufficient to provide the needed food supplies, the rear

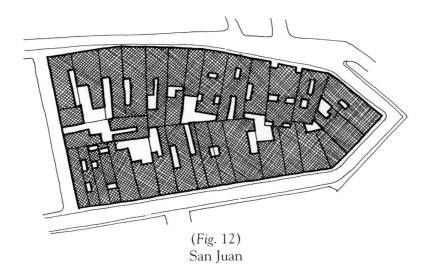

(*Fig.* 12)
San Juan

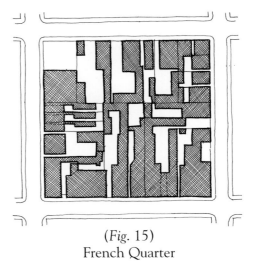

(*Fig.* 15)
French Quarter

57

yard was no longer necessary for food production and the land became more valuable for housing and commercial use. In response, as was experienced throughout Europe some five hundred years earlier, the character of the Quarter changed drastically. Lots were subdivided, typically in half, resulting in lots with a pronounced proportion—narrow and deep. Soon, two- and three-story attached townhouses were being constructed and the Quarter began to take on the urban character in evidence today.

The new attached townhouses, constructed on the front property line, housed shops at the first level and living quarters on the upper levels, very similar to those in the major cities of Europe at the time. Access to a rear courtyard was through a passageway (porte cochère)—the courtyard was formed by a service wing housing a kitchen, servants' quarters, and garçonniére, and extended from the main structure along one side of the property. In some cases, the service wing wrapped around to the rear property line. The resulting courtyards provided privacy, outdoor living, and workspace with access to slave quarters, privies, washrooms, kitchens, and stables, which, in the heat of the summer, must have resulted in much sensory unpleasantness.

As to the question raised earlier, of whether the courtyards in the Quarter are of Spanish or French origin, neither culture can claim authorship. The Spanish were the first to construct courtyard houses in the New World because they were the first to colonize the New World. It is safe to assume that had the French or English proceeded the Spanish, they, too, would most likely have chosen this house form, and it can be demonstrated that in both French and English West Indian settlements, as they matured from small villages to urban centers, courtyards were common. And to further argue the concept of a cross-cultural borrowing of ideas, there was a townhouse very similar to a Creole townhouse constructed in the British-influenced city of Baltimore in 1760, thirty-five years before one was ever constructed in New Orleans. A more plausible explanation for the popularity of the courtyards in the Quarter is that they provided solutions to problems that existed at a particular time in a particular place, an idea realized by both French and Spanish citizens after the fire of 1794. In the words of Jay Edwards, "In the case of New Orleans, Spanish culture provided an inspiration, French culture a model."

BUILDING TYPES & STYLES

As the new city emerged, the major building types were Creole cottages, outbuildings (generally constructed in the rear of Creole cottages), and townhouses.

The most common style of the period is most accurately referred to as Creole, a blending of French and Spanish characteristics evolved in the West Indies and matured in colonial Louisiana. While some distinctive Spanish colonial buildings were constructed, primarily with flat-tiled terrace roofs, the majority of the buildings continued the French traditions.

Creole Cottages

The urban Creole cottages of the French Quarter are rectangular buildings with a foursquare room arrangement and a side gable roof, a design that provided more usable attic space. Creole cottages supplanted Norman cottages after the great fires; however, raised Creole cottages with front galleries and Norman cottages continued to be constructed in the rural areas of the Louisiana colony.

The inspiration for the urban Creole cottage most likely came from Cap-Haïten, for very similar houses can be found there. However, side-gabled cottages were also common in Spanish colonial settlements. Constructed low to the ground, Creole cottages were generally situated on the front property line, abutting the sidewalk. They were most often detached structures with a narrow alley on one or both sides leading to a rear courtyard, where two- or three-story detached outbuildings, constructed on the rear property line, housed kitchens and servants quarters.

The typical plan consists of four rooms with rear cabinets flanking a loggia. Ceiling heights were low, and steep roofs, covered with tiles or shingles, with an overhanging roof or *abat vent*—a separate awning-like projection—protected the sidewalk and the front wall of the house from sun and rain. The two front rooms faced the street. Each had one door and one window, and the house had two fireplaces, each serving two rooms. Although less common, the Quarter has a number

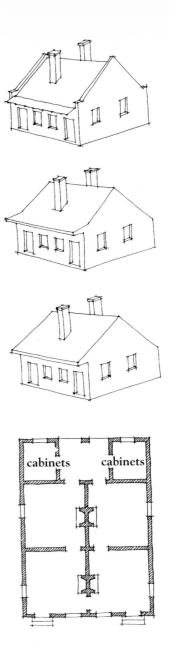

cabinets   cabinets

59

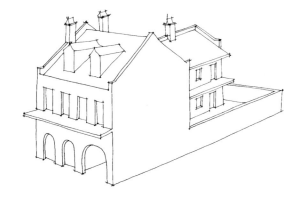

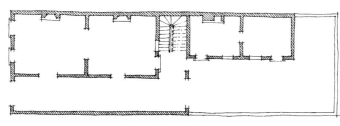

First-Floor Plan

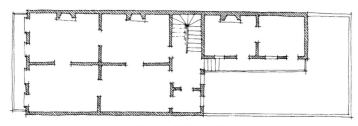

Second-Floor Plan

of two-bay Creole cottages, a building whose plan is one-half of a typical Creole cottage.

The majority of the Quarter's Creole cottages is located beyond Royal Street, as was the case as described in the journals of Benjamin Latrobe in 1819:

"The roofs are high, covered with tiles or shingles, and project five feet over the footway, which is also five feet wide. The eaves therefore discharge the water into the Gutters. However different this mode is, from the American manner of building, it has very great advantages both with regard to the interior of the dwelling, and to the street. In the Summer the walls are perfectly shaded from the Sun, and the house kept cool, while the passengers are also shaded from the Sun, and protected from the rain. From my lodgings to Mr. Nolte's is a distance 650 feet independently of the crossing of two streets, and yet in the heaviest rains I can walk to his house perfectly dry excepting for about 200 feet in front of a dead Wall and some high houses in Thoulouse street."

Townhouses

The four most common types of townhouses constructed in the Quarter during this period were the porte cochère, the hotel, the Creole townhouse, and the entresol house.

PORTE COCHÈRE TOWNHOUSE

The porte cochère townhouse provides an efficient use of space, as it provides access to the rear courtyard through a carriageway while allowing the upper levels extend above the carriageway to the full width of the property. Townhouses with side gable roofs could be placed side-by-side, forming a continuous facade at the street. The rear courtyard, accessed by the porte cochère, was protected from the view of neighbors by a tall, brick, windowless wall that formed the adjacent *garçonnière* In the courtyard could be found stables, a kitchen, a wash building, and a privy. It also served as outdoor workspace, as well as a place for social gatherings.

The *hotel*, derives its name from a similar urban house type found in seventeenth-century Paris. It is similar to the above-described porte cochère townhouse, except that the porte cochère is centrally located instead of being located on one side of the house. These houses required wider lots than the porte cochère townhouses, and consequently, they were usually of a grander scale and had a more pronounced street presence.

CREOLE TOWNHOUSE

The Creole townhouse is similar to the porte cochère townhouse described above, except that the passage from the sidewalk to the rear courtyard is too narrow for carriages and is only for pedestrians (*fig.* 16).

ENTRESOL TOWNHOUSE

The entresol townhouse is a building with a commercial use at the first floor, storage at the second, and residential above. At the time of their appearance in New Orleans, they were common in Havana (the principal Spanish port with which New Orleans traded during this time) as well as Paris (*fig.* 17).

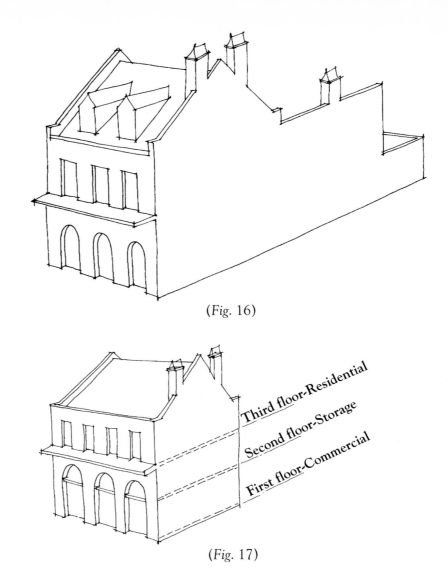

(*Fig.* 16)

(*Fig.* 17)

Third floor-Residential
Second floor-Storage
First floor-Commercial

61

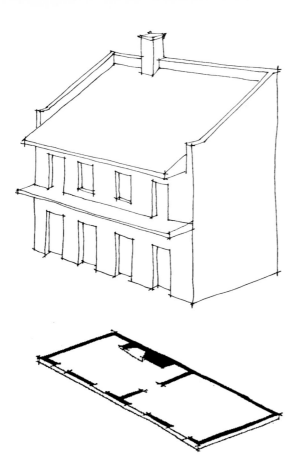

OUTBUILDINGS

Outbuildings were most commonly constructed in the rear yards of Creole cottages and Creole townhouses. Generally two or three stories in height, these service buildings were most often built of brick and had a narrow, cantilevered gallery used for passage at the upper level(s), with slender wooden colonnettes supporting a shed roof sloping into the courtyard.

The first level housed the kitchen and servants' quarters, while the upper level(s) provided quarters for servants or the young men in the family, who were allowed greater independence and privacy than the young women who, by contrast, were required to live in the main house. The separation of the kitchen from the main residence kept the heat generated by cooking out of the house and also isolated the main house from the treat of fire associated with kitchens.

Paris, France

French Quarter

French Quarter

Havana, Cuba
(Spanish)

French Quarter

French Quarter

Fort de France, Martinique
(French)

French Quarter

French Quarter

WROUGHT IRON

A prominent characteristic of the Quarter, wrought iron was introduced in the late Spanish colonial era and remained popular until the introduction of cast iron around 1850. Wrought iron differs from cast iron in that its carbon content is much less, allowing it to be shaped and assembled by hand. Cast iron, by contrast, is cast in a mold. Wrought iron in the Quarter had numerous influences; historical traditions of the French, Spanish, and English all made contributions.

Iron has its origins in the Asia Minor as early as 1500 B.C. The Romans spread the use of ironwork as they expanded their empire, but after the fall, its use declined drastically. France and England were left with many relics from the Roman domination, but it was not until the eleventh century that they experienced an awakening of their ironwork tradition. Roman antiquity had also left its imprint on Spain, and the first significant Spanish revival of ironwork surfaced in the twelfth century, exhibiting many similarities to the work of the French and English. During the next two centuries, ironwork in Europe enjoyed a slow increase in popularity. Under the influence of the Moors, Spanish ironwork gradually matured, resulting in a blending of Gothic (a French innovation) and Moorish influences, creating the "Mudéjar" style.

By the beginning of the fourteenth century, the Renaissance in Italy began to exhibit a profound influence throughout Europe, and from the middle of the 1400s to the early part of the 1500s, Spain experienced its most brilliant era of wrought iron—the result of a blending of the Mudéjar style with Italian Renaissance influences. Alive with prosperity and adventure, the Spanish directed their wealth to the construction of massive cathedrals and churches adorned with elaborate iron grilles, unequalled before or since. (Geerlings 1983)

During the Renaissance, English ironwork assumed many of the mannerisms of cast iron, and by the middle of the 1600s, ironwork balconies were common throughout England. By the late eighteenth century, the work of the Adam brothers dominated English architectural fashion, exhibiting a combination of cast and wrought iron.

French ironwork enjoyed a slow evolution, but in the seventeenth century, under the reign of Louis XIII, the baroque era fueled innovation. By the late seventeenth century, French artistic influence was widespread on the greater part of the European continent, culminating in the excesses of the rococo in the eighteenth century.

In Spain, balconies with wrought-iron railings became universal, often extending across entire facades composed of spindles and supported by long, graceful scrolls. The designs used by the Spanish were typically French. Gerald K. Geerlings states that, "Although at certain periods Italian, Spanish, and English craftsmanship ascended loftier summits in iron work than did the French, nevertheless the latter's influence and superiority continued for longer periods than any of the others.

Wrought iron had very limited use in New Orleans during the French colonial era, primarily because most of the French colonial buildings had no galleries or were constructed of wood whereby wooden columns and balustrades were utilized. During the Spanish dominion, after the fires, the use of wrought iron evolved, primarily used with buildings constructed of brick. For houses, as well as public buildings, it was used for fences, gates, and balcony railings, (which frequently incorporated a monogram into the design) and as a result, wrought iron in New Orleans has come to be associated with the Spanish culture. Its appearance during this period, however, is more closely associated with timing than with culture, since wrought iron was also common at the time in France, England, and throughout Europe; and its use became popular in the West Indian colonies of all three major powers simultaneously. Generally speaking, the ironwork styles of the French, Spanish, and English West Indian colonies are indistinguishable, more evidence of the significance of cross-cultural blending in the colonial era.

GABRIEL PEYROUX HOUSE

901-07 Burgundy
Circa 1780

Constructed around 1780, the Gabriel Peyroux House is a good example of a simple West Indian cottage, a type common in Louisiana during this period. The house, owned by Gabriel Peyroux, was moved to this site from Peyroux's plantation on Bayou Road by Mauricio Milon in 1781. In its original state, the house was surrounded by galleries and raised above the ground on brick piers, as was the tradition for most rural buildings of the period.

Rectangular in form, with a slate-covered hip roof, the house presently exposes its brique-entre-poteaux construction. Originally, this underbody was clad in horizontally laid weatherboard. In recent years, and with current technology which allows for adequate waterproofing, the weatherboard has been removed, the brique-entre-poteaux has been exposed, and the result is undoubtedly charming. Interestingly, at that time, this construction technique and resulting appearance was common in Normandy, France, the source of inspiration for much of the French colonial architecture of early New Orleans.

MERIEULT HOUSE

527-533 Royal Street
Circa 1792
National Historic Landmark

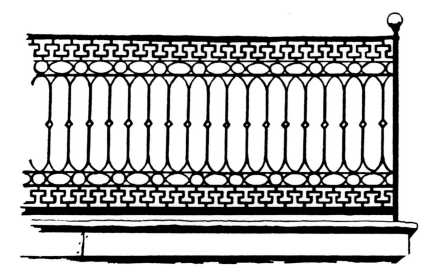

The Mirieult House was constructed for Jean François Merieult, a merchant-trader, around 1792 on the site of the first barracks, forges, and workshops of the Company of the Indies. The house incorporates part for the Guinalt House, constructed in the 1750s, and was one of the few buildings to survive the fire of 1794. It underwent extensive renovation in the style of the 1830s for Manuel J. de Lizardi, at which time the ground floor openings were modified with the addition of the granite columns.

The house was operated as a hotel, The Royal House, by the Trapolin family, who owned it from 1878 to 1938. In 1938, it was restored for Gen. and Mrs. L. Kemper Williams by architect Richard Koch. Since 1966 it has been the home of the Historic New Orleans Collection, and the house is open to the public.

MONTEGUT HOUSE

731 Royal Street
Circa 1795

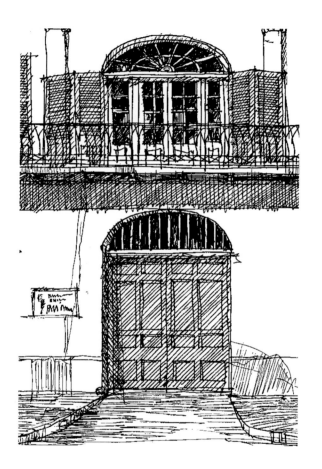

The Montegut House was constructed shortly after the fire of 1794 for Dr. Joseph Montegut, the surgeon-major of the Spanish army and chef surgeon at the old Charity Hospital. A one-story wing was constructed in the rear in 1796 after Gilberto Guillemard's 1790 design. During their exile from France, the Duke of Orleans and his two brothers were entertained by Dr. Montegut at this house. The duke became the godfather of one of Dr. Montegut's daughters.

The house is a five-bay, hotel-townhouse with a central porte cochère leading to a rear courtyard. The stuccoed, front facade features a fanlighted central entrance, which is repeated at the second level. The openings at the first level are arched, with French doors and arched fanlights.

The roof is pierced by three segmentally arched dormers.

Lloyd Vogt

CREOLE COTTAGES

625-627 & 629 Burgundy Street
Circa 1810

The date of construction of these two houses is unknown—research indicates that they were constructed between 1808 and 1821, at which time they were owned by Pierre Seuzeneau, who died in 1821.

The land on which these houses stand was originally the St. Peter Street Cemetery (1721-1788), the first cemetery in the city. After the major flood, fire, and epidemic of 1788, the Cabildo ordered the cemetery closed, constructing St. Louis Cemetery Number One on Rampart Street.

These houses are good examples of the Creole cottages of the period. The house on the left is a typical four-bay cottage, while the smaller one on the right is a two-bay, "half" Creole cottage. With stuccoed facades, each has five walls extending above the roof on the sides and a metal *abat vent* extending over the sidewalk. Similar picturesque cottages can be found scattered throughout the Quarter.

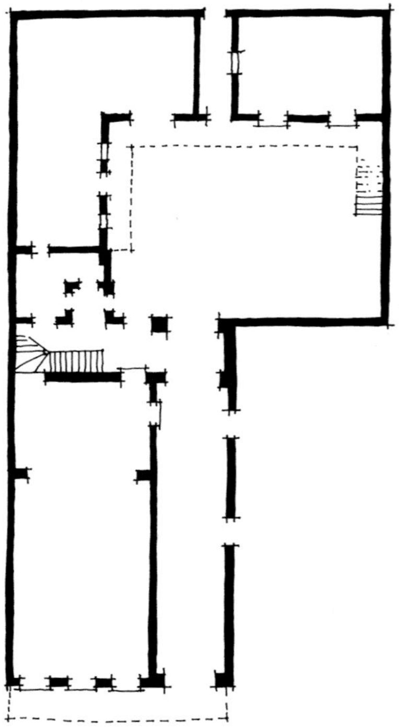

BARTHOLOME BOSQUE HOUSE

617 Chartres Street
1795

First Floor

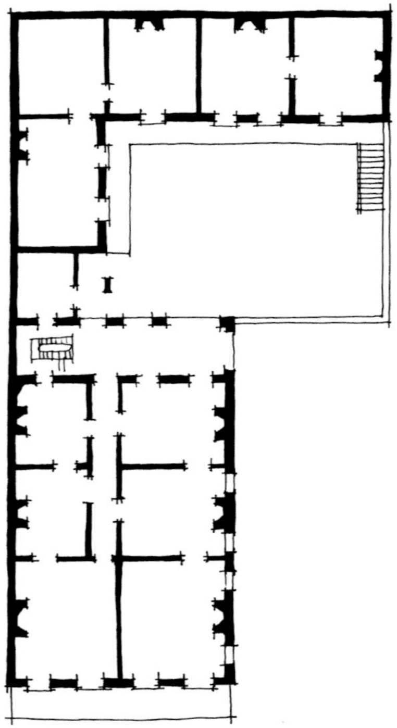

Second Floor

While on this site stands an important colonial building, the site itself may be more infamous than the building, for on this site on Good Friday, March 21, 1788, the first of the two devastating French Quarter fires began. In 1795, a year after the second fire, the Bosque House was constructed. It is the first recorded porte cochère townhouse in New Orleans.

The house was built by Bartholome Bosque, a Spanish-born shipowner and merchant, and the architect was most likely Barthelemy Lafon, one of the best-known architect-builders of the time. Initially constructed with a very low-pitched rooftop terrace in the Spanish style, after experiencing the heavy rains so common in New Orleans, the flat roof was replaced with a more watertight, steeper-pitched tile roof.

The front facade of the building has been altered somewhat. Originally, the first-floor openings would have been similar to the second-floor windows in scale and character. The large, glass, shop windows now in place, separated with large cast-iron columns, were added in the nineteenth century. In addition, the original gallery was probably narrower than the current gallery, supported on columns extending over the sidewalk.

A spacious carriageway leads to a rear courtyard, kitchen, and servants' quarters. The first floor, facing the street, houses shops, and a stair hall entered from a rear loggia leads up to the dwelling at the second level. Four French doors open onto a second-level balcony with wrought-iron railings projecting over the sidewalk, a characteristic most likely first introduced to New Orleans with this house.

ORUE-PONTALBA HOUSE

Le Petit Theatre du Vieux Carré
600 St. Peter Street
1789-1795

This house has experienced many reincarnations in form as well as function. The house was first built in 1789 for the head financial accountant of the Spanish Royal Army, Don Josef de Orue y Garbea. The architect was Gilberto Guillemard and the builder was Hilaire Boutte. The house was severely damaged in the fire of 1794, and soon thereafter, Josef Xavier Delfau de Pontalba purchased the house and rebuilt it for his aunt Celest Macarty, widow of Don Esteban Miro, governor of Louisiana from 1785 to 1791.

During the nineteenth century, a series of tenants, about which not much is known, occupied the upper residential portions of the house, while the ground floor housed a tavern called Le Veau qui Tete, or The Sucking Calf, then the Cafe de La Louisiane, and finally, it became the Louisiana Exchange.

Although the living conditions in the Quarter declined in the latter part of the nineteenth century, by the 1920s, it began to experience an economic renaissance. Allured by an ambience of romance and intrigue, artists, musicians, and writers were drawn to the Quarter and occupied the older structures. One such group was Le Petit Theatre. Founded shortly after World War I, this group began meeting in the uptown homes of its members to read plays in both English and French, and in 1922, they purchased the building and built a theater and connecting loggia. The presence of this prestigious group reinforced the growing interest in the Quarter and ushered in a romantic renaissance. The new theater, designed by New Orleans architectural firm Armstrong & Koch, was sensitive to the adjacent historic properties and represents one of the first attempts to build a modern building in the traditional style of the quarter.

In 1963, the building was determined to be unsafe and architects Richard Koch & Samuel Wilson designed the existing building using Guillemard's original building specifications and the earliest available photographs as documentation.

722 TOULOUSE STREET

Circa 1788

While the actual date of this house is unknown, research conducted by Samuel Wilson, Jr., indicates that it was most likely constructed in 1788. While it has lost its outbuildings in the rear, the house apparently escaped destruction in the fire of 1794.

Constructed for Louis Adam, the house was sold by his widow, Dame Louise de Beon, to Jean Baptiste Sainet in 1805. The same year, Sainet sold the house to Louis D'Aquin, who, four months later, sold it to Joseph Guillot. Gurlie and Guillot made modifications to the house in 1805.

The house was constructed in the Spanish colonial era and reflects the attitude of the period. At the second level, the cantilevered wooden balcony with a simple wooden balustrade is supported by wrought-iron brackets. The clay-barrel tile roof is supported by slender, turned, wooden colonnettes. A small, centrally located dormer articulates the front facade. Batten shutters protected the lower-level openings, while louvered shutters are used on the four French doors opening into the balcony.

The house has been restored to its late Spanish colonial appearance by the Historic New Orleans Collection.

PEDESCLAUX-LEMONNIER HOUSE

640 Royal Street
1795-1811

Although formally referred to as the Pedesclaux-LeMonnier house, this building is also known by several names descriptive of owners, legends, and literary characters. Pierre Pedesclaux, one of the best-known notaries in New Orleans, under Spanish and American rule, lived on the property in a small one-story building, giving the house its first known name. The construction of the building was started after the designs of Barthèlèmy Lafon.

A physician, Yves LeMonnier and apothecary Francois Grandchamps purchased the building at a public auction and the house was completed in 1811 after designs by LaCarriere Latour and Hyacinth LaClotte. LeMonnier purchased the entire house in 1821. It remained his family home for fifty years (Toledano 1996).

The house contained four shops on the ground floor, six rooms on the second floor, seven rooms on the third floor, garden-terraced roof, and a rear courtyard. The third-floor wrought-iron balcony design incorporates the doctor's initials YLM.

Because of its height, the house has also come to be known as "The Skyscraper Building." Any house taller than two stories was uncommon at the time, and residents of the Quarter doubted that the soft New Orleans soil could support a third story. It is said that for a period of time, people were reluctant to walk down the street and carriages would not drive in front of the house, fearing that vibrations would unsettle the building and send it toppling over.

In 1876, long after the residents' fears of collapse were put to rest, Betrand Saloy, a merchant, bought the house, added the fourth story, and turned the building into a tenement. It was in this setting that the American novelist George W. Cable placed his celebrated fictional character, Sieur George.

Third-Floor Plan

Lloyd Vogt

BANQUE DE LA LOUISIANE

Brennan's Restaurant
417 Royal Street
1795

Built in 1795, the Banque de la Louisiane was constructed by Vincent Rillieux, great grandfather of the artist Edgar Degas. Rillieux purchased the site shortly after the December 8, 1794 fire destroyed the earlier buildings that had stood there.

In 1805 the building was bought to house the Banque de la Louisiane, the first bank established in New Orleans after the Louisiana Purchase. From 1841 to 1891, the building served as a residence for the Alonzo Morphy family, whose son, Paul Morphy, (born 1837) became a world chess champion. He died in the house in 1884. In 1920 the building was given to Tulane University by William Ratcliffe Irby and in 1955 became Brennan's Restaurant, which it is to this day.

The building is a two-story, stuccoed structure with a porte cochère that leads to a rear courtyard.

SAINT LOUIS CATHEDRAL
(Replaced by the Cathedral of 1850)

Jackson Square
1794

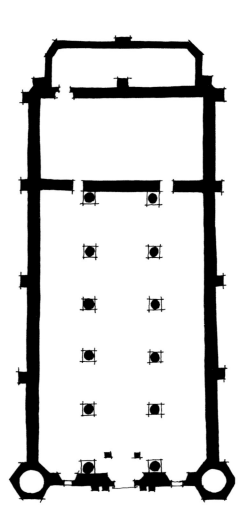

The Spanish cathedral illustrated here was designed as part of the ensemble of the Cabildo and Presbytère. It was designed in 1789 by architect Gilberto Guillemard and was financed by the Patron Andrés Almonester y Roxas, after the devastating fire of 1788 destroyed the old church. It was dedicated as a cathedral on Christmas Eve in 1794.

Gilberto Guillemard (1746-1808), born in France, was trained in mathematics and military design. He served as an engineer in the service of Spain at Baton Rouge, Mobile, and Pensacola, before coming to New Orleans around 1770.

The building introduced classical forms to New Orleans and recalled designs of colonial churches of Mexico and Spanish South America. It features a central, classically inspired portico flanked by two towers. This basic form was originated by Italian Renaissance architects, as they combined the Italian, classical, central portico with the towers of the French Gothic cathedrals. In 1820 the cathedral was altered by an addition of a central tower by Benjamin H. Latrobe, who, of English training, was no doubt influenced by the central spired churches of Sir Christopher Wren in England in the late 1600s.

The building underwent extensive renovation by J. N. B. dePouilly in the 1840s. It was replaced by the present-day cathedral in 1850, after the collapse of the belfry.

THE CABILDO

Jackson Square
1795-1799
National Historic Landmark

Cabildo is the Spanish term for the Spanish governing body—the Spanish Cabildo is the municipal building of that body. The Cabildo in New Orleans was conceived by architect Gilberto Guillemard for Patron Andrés Almonester y Roxas as part of an ensemble consisting of the Cabildo, the St. Louis Cathedral, and the Presbytère.

The design of the building has a strong Spanish influence, as noted by architectural historian Talbot Hamlin, recalling the facade of the Cabildo in Oaxaca, Mexico, built around 1780. The arched arcade is a common feature of municipal buildings fronting the plaza of Span-ish colonial settlements, as was dictated in the *Laws of the Indies,* which served as guidelines for Spanish colonial settlements in the New World. The Cabildo incorporates portions of the Corps de Garde, constructed in 1750, remaining from the devastating fire of 1794. The ornate wrought-iron balcony rails were executed locally by Marcellino Hernandez.

The building was completed just at the time of the transfer of the Louisiana Territory to the United States. Here, on December 20, 1803, the official transfer was executed, and soon thereafter, the building became the American City Hall, serving the city in that capacity until 1853, when it became the building of the Supreme Court of Louisiana until 1910. Originally, the building had a flat-tiled terrace roof, in the Spanish tradition. In 1847, a mansard roof with habitable attic was added, under the direction of Louis Surgi, city surveyor, and replaced the original flat-tiled terrace roof.

Since 1911 the building has been owned and operated by the Louisiana State Museum. The building was designated a national historic landmark in 1960.

PRESBYTÈRE

Jackson Square
1798-1813
National Historic Landmark

The Presbytère, flanking the St. Louis Cathedral to the right, was designed by Gilberto Guillemard on the site where the parsonage was located before being destroyed in the fire of 1788. It was designed as part of the ensemble of the St. Louis Cathedral and the Cabildo (which flanks the cathedral to the left), which was being financed by Andrés Almonester y Roxas. When Roxas died in 1798, only the first floor of the structure was completed. His death interrupted the construction, and a temporary roof was constructed to stabilize the partially completed building.

In 1813, construction continued and the building was completed by builders Claude Gurlie and Joseph Guillot. In 1840 it was enlarged by Benjamin Buisson, and in 1847, a mansard roof was added, to match the Cabildo, by Henri Gobet and Victor Amiel, builders. The building is almost identical, in exterior appearance, to the Cabildo.

Although originally intended to serve as the rectory (Casa Curial) of the St. Louis Cathedral, it was never used for this purpose. Through the years, the building was rented for, and then sold to, the city as a courthouse, a store, and as apartments. The building has been owned and operated by the Louisiana State Museum since 1911. It was designated a national historic landmark in 1970.

DE LA TORRE HOUSE

707-709 Dumaine Street
Circa 1800

While a number of cottages were built with flat-terrace roofs during this era, 707-709 Dumaine Street is the only one left unaltered. The front facade has four openings, two doors with two windows between, and a parapet comprised of half-round, Spanish tiles between end-stucco pillars. It is part of a row of three buildings built in 1800 by Majeur de Brigade de Garde Joachim de La Torre shortly after his purchase of the property from Barthélémy Lafon, an architect-surveyor, who most likely designed the buildings.

The flat roof exhibited here was common in the Spanish colonial era after the two great fires. The roofs of these houses were used as terraces, where the women of the house washed and ironed and the men walked from house to house for roof-terrace socializing with neighbors.

Because of the subtropical New Orleans climate, with sixty inches of rain yearly, waterproofing these flat roofs proved problematic; and one by one, through the years, to these flat-roofed houses of the Quarter, remnants of Spanish tradition, were added pitched roofs in the French tradition, as can be seen today.

THE END OF AN ERA

In the late 1700s, Louisiana began to develop an agricultural economy. Indigo and cotton were encouraged as cash crops, wheat, corn, and rice as food crops. Sawmills grew in number, scattered throughout the colony, and tobacco was processed and packed for export. Sugarcane, first grown in Louisiana as a curiosity, became one of the area's most important money crops after Étienne de Boré discovered the process of granulating cane to produce sugar in 1795. Expert sugar makers were imported from Saint-Domingue to guide the growth of the new industry, and within eight years, there were seventy-five sugar mills on the Mississippi River, producing five million pounds of sugar a year.

By 1790, the African population in New Orleans had reached approximately 2,500 in number, equivalent to whites, and their influence was being felt. Lyle Saxon tells us: "It is likely that from the very beginning of the colony in 1718, African superstitions had given trouble to the colonists . . . In any event, voodooism was firmly implanted in early Colonial New Orleans, and it was not long before white men and women felt its power and learned to fear it . . . By the end of the eighteenth century, voodooism was firmly entrenched. This secret society extended through the entire slave population and among the free negroes as well."

Fueled by the flames of the French Revolution, slave unrest erupted into revolution in Saint-Domingue in 1792. The exodus of the colony by the whites, free persons of color, and slaves started shortly thereafter. Fleeing in all directions, some, but not a large number, came to Louisiana in the early years. Between 1798 and 1803, the largest exile occurred, with the majority (over 25,000) migrating to the southeast coast of Cuba—most of whom would eventually end up in Louisiana. The character of New Orleans, with each introduction of a new culture, continued to diversify and blend, a process that would eventually result in its unique cultural identity.

As the economy grew, so did the need for labor, and the number of slaves grew dramatically. During this time, Louisiana's population of free people of color also grew, enabling them to mature into a community and achieve political importance. Increase of the native population and the ease with which manumission was accomplished under Spanish administration, along with the influx of free blacks from Saint-Domingue, increased the number of free people of color in the colony from 165 at the end of the French era to almost 1,500 by the end of the Spanish dominion (Hirsch 1992).

In 1800, part of Napoleon's plan for a new French empire in Louisiana was executed, and the territory was returned to France by the Treaty of San Ildefonso, a treaty which was kept secret for over two years. When Spain acquired Louisiana in 1762, it was a small, weak, unprofitable colony with a population of scarcely 7,500. At the end of the Spanish rule, some forty years later, it was a prosperous colony of more than 50,000 people, about 30,000 of whom lived in New Orleans.

Although the Spanish controlled New Orleans for thirty-seven years, in large part because they allowed and encouraged the preservation of the French-Creole language, culture, and traditions, the city remained essentially French. In the words of Sam Wilson, Jr.:

> "For the first fifty years of its existence as a city, New Orleans was entirely a French town under the fleur-de-lys of Bourbon France. Although these early years were marked by difficulties, frustrations and slow growth, the half century under the rule of her French founders left and indelible imprint upon the city, leaving it a character that is unique among all other cities of the United States. Its dominant culture, tradition, and language remained French even after it passed into the hands of Spain and finally became part of the United States with the Louisiana Purchase in 1803."

The Spanish who came to New Orleans found themselves far more changed by the city than they were able to change it—like so many others who came, they became New Orleanians. Nevertheless, it is to Spain, and not France, that the region owes the greatest debt for its colonial development.

THE FEDERAL PERIOD
1803—1835

Louisiana
Territory

IN 1803, THE FORMAL TRANSFER of the Louisiana Territory from Spain back to France was executed. By this time, President Jefferson was far along in his efforts to negotiate the purchase of Louisiana by the United States. On April 30, 1803, the Louisiana Purchase Treaty was signed, bringing to an end Louisiana's colonial era—it was now under the control of the United States.

On December 20, 1803, in a ceremony that took place on the balcony of the Cabildo, overlooking the Place d'Armes, Louisiana was formally transferred to the United States. New Orleans, at the time, was home to approximately 8,000, a population made up of Frenchmen, Spaniards, Americans, Germans, Indians, and Africans, both slave and free, who comprised nearly half of the total.

THE EARLY PERIOD: 1803-1820

For a number of years prior to the Louisiana Purchase, frontiersman from the northern American territories had been traveling down the Mississippi in keelboats to sell cornmeal, pickled pork, and whiskey. While the Creoles traded with the frontiersman, they did not socialize with them, as they considered their culture superior to that of the Americans, most of whom they considered riverboat roughnecks. The upper classes of Creole society initially remained in control of the economy and politics. However, New Orleans was a city of great opportunity for men of all classes, and it was not long before the number of Americans entering the city, in search of work as well as fortunes in the cotton and river trades, began to increase. Separated by nationality, language, religion, traditions, laws, and politics, interaction between the established Creoles and the arriving Americans was strained at best, as it was becoming clear that the American influence would eventually become a powerful force in New Orleans.

In 1808, the Saint-Dominique refugees, who had settled in Cuba after fleeing the slave revolutions, were expelled by the Spanish military, once more to be uprooted. By 1809, shiploads of Saint-Domingue refugees began arriving at the port of New Orleans. In a two-year period, over 9,000 migrated to Louisiana—approximately 2,700 whites, 3,100 free persons of color, and 3,200 slaves. By 1815, over 11,000 had arrived, most of whom remained in New Orleans.

Fearing the economic competition from the wave of Americans entering Louisiana, the locals welcomed this influx of French-speaking Creoles, whose presence doubled the city's population. The culture and class structure of New Orleans bore great resemblance to the tri-caste model of the refugees, who came from all three castes. Their civil laws were identical and they were drawn together by language, blood, affinity, and a long history of interaction, both social and economic. Their contributions to the culture of the city are well documented. They were instrumental in energizing local newspapers, opera, theater, pharmacies, music schools, and the book trade, while

95

reinforcing the French-Spanish Creole culture and building traditions. In some respects, Saint-Domingue had given birth to Louisiana and sustained her to maturation. It was fitting that the Saint-Domingueas, when displaced, sought refuge with a close member of the Creole family.

By 1810, expanded by the Saint-Domingue immigrants, the population of New Orleans had grown to over 17,000, making it the fifth-largest city in the United States, behind New York, Philadelphia, Baltimore, and Boston. In that same year, under direction from the east coast by Benjamin Henry Latrobe, the city developed its first waterworks system, consisting of a network of hollow, cypress logs through which river water was pumped. Latrobe was a prominent Philadelphia architect who had served as the architect of the U.S. Capital and designed the first building in America to employ a Greek order (the Bank of Philadelphia), launching the Greek revival era in America. Although the system operated as was intended, the majority of the population continued to use rainwater collected off of roofs into cisterns.

The first steamboat arrived in New Orleans in 1812, and on April 30 of that same year, Louisiana became America's eighteenth state. By now the levee had become a bustling open-air market. Benjamin Latrobe describes his experiences as he arrives in New Orleans in January of 1819.

"The strange and loud noise heard through the fog, on board the *Clio*, proceeding from the voices of the Market people and their customers was not more extraordinary than the appearance of these noisy folks when the fog cleared away, and we landed. Every thing had an *odd* look. For 25 Years I have been a traveler only between New York and Richmond, and I confess that I felt myself in some degree, again a Cockney, for it was impossible not to stare, at a sight wholly new even to one who had travelled much in Europe and America.

The first remarkable appearance was that of the Market Boats, differing in form and equipment from any thing that floats on the Atlantic side of our country.

At the top of the flight we arrived on the Levee extending along the front of the city. It is a wide Bank of earth, level on the top to the width of perhaps 50 feet, and thence sloping gradually, in a very easy descent to the foot way or banquet at the houses, a distance of about 150 to 200 feet from the edge of the Levee. This foot way is about 5 feet below the level of the Levee, of course 4 feet below the Surface of the Water in the river at the time of the inundation, which rises within one foot, sometimes less, of the top of the Levee.

Along the Levee, as far as the eye could reach to the West, and to the Market house to the East were ranged two rows of Market people, some having stalls or tables with a Tilt or awning of Canvass, but the Majority having their wares lying on the ground, perhaps on a piece of canvass, or a parcel of Palmetto leaves. The articles to be sold were not more various than the sellers. White Men and women, and of all hues of brown, and of all Classes of faces, from round Yankees, to grisly and lean Spaniards, black Negroes and negresses filthy Indians half naked, Mulattoes, curly and straight haired, Quateroons of all shades long haired and frizzled, the women dressed in the most flaring yellow, and scarlet gowns, the men capped and hatted.

Their wares consisted of as many kinds as their faces. Innumerable wild ducks, Oysters, poultry of all kinds, fish, bananas, piles of Oranges, Sugar Cane, sweet and Irish potatoes, corn in the Ear and husked, apples, carrots and all sorts of other roots, eggs, trinkets, tin ware, dry goods, in fact of more and odder things to be sold in the manner and place, than I can enumerate. The market was full of wretched beef and other butchers meat, and some excellent and large fish. I cannot suppose that my eye took in less than 500 sellers and buyers, all of whom appeared to strain their voices, to exceed each other in loudness. A little further along the Levee on the margin of a heap of bricks, was a bookseller whose stocks of books, English and French cut no mean appearance."

New Orleans was growing and so was the economy.

BUILDING TYPES & STYLES

Townhouses and Creole cottages, popular in the late colonial era, continued to be the house types of choice in the early federal period. The Creole style continued to be the style of choice until the 1820s, at which time American influence, as the result of the rapidly growing American population, began to shift the aesthetic taste of the populace toward classical idioms common in the English colonies throughout the colonial era.

97

ABSINTHE HOUSE

238 Bourbon Street
1806

Located on the corner of Bourbon and Bienville Streets, no building in the Quarter has had more stories told about it than the Absinthe House. It earned its name from the potent green drink made from wormwood that has been served from the bar for the past century. The building was erected by Pedro Font and Francisco Juncadella, soon after Juncadella purchased the corner site from Dame Marie Car on March 23, 1806. Font and Juncadella converted the lower floor into an epicurean food depot and the upper floors into a residence. They imported foodstuffs, wine, and other goods from their native Barcelona, Spain and called the establishment "Front and Juncadella."

After Juncadella's death, his widow and Pedro Font returned to Spain, leaving the store to be run by their relatives, Jacinto, Leopold, and P. O. Aleix. In 1838, the structure housed a shoe shop; in 1843, a grocery store; and in 1861, a coffeehouse. In 1870 they employed Cayetano Ferrér, a Catalan from Barcelona, as bartender. Cayetano had come to New Orleans several years before and worked as a bartender in the basement bar of the old French Opera House. In 1874, he took over the lease of the building and it became known as the "Absinthe Room," where he created the frapped green liquid, Absinthe (the establishment's specialty), which gained national notoriety. The recipe for absinthe was a closely held secret and was never successfully duplicated by competing bars.

The entire Ferrér family—father, mother, Uncle Leon, and three sons, Felix, Paul, and Jacinto—continued to serve customers in what became "The Old Absinthe Room." In 1886 Cayetano died and Ferrér's widow and sons continued the business. From around 1890, it became known as the "Old Absinthe House."

LA RIONDA-CORREJOLLES HOUSE

1218-1220 Burgundy Street
Circa 1810

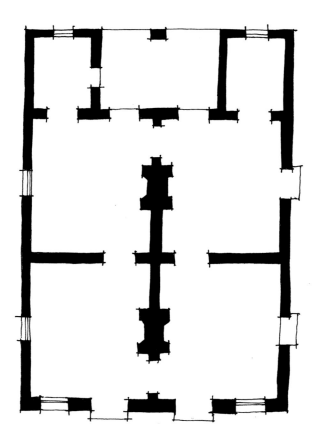

The La Rionda cottage was constructed by José Antonio La Rionda, or as the Spanish name appears in the French act of sale from 1810, Joseph de La Rionda. The lot was sold by Louis Dufilho. La Rionda constructed the house, and most likely a second one very similar, as rental or for-sale properties. Because of financial difficulties, he was forced to sell the house at a public auction in 1812, at which time it was purchased by Madame Jeanne Elizabeth Berguin, a recent widow of Jean Joseph Louis Rousset. Shortly after purchasing the house, Jeanne Elizabeth married Jean Quessart, the elder. From the small buildings in the rear of the house, Madame Quessart, with the younger brother of her husband, Jean, operated a chocolate and tobacco factory. The house, along with the factory, was sold at auction in 1828, after the yellow fever epidemic of that year took the life of both Jeanne Elizabeth and Jean.

The plan of the house is that of a typical Creole cottage of the period, having four rooms with double fireplaces between the two front and two rear rooms, and a rear loggia flanked by two cabinets. The front facade has a typical pattern of four openings—window, French door, French door, window. Many cottages from this period had the alternative relationship—two centrally located windows flanked by French doors.

Except for the roof, which was originally tile and has been replaced with slate, the house appears today very much as it did when it was constructed.

FRENCH MARKET

Decatur Street
1813-1823

The site of the French Market, on the banks of the Mississippi River, was once used by American Indians as a bartering place. The first market structure was built by the Spanish in 1791. It was later replaced. Consisting of a complex of buildings, the oldest existing structures are located at 800 Decatur Street (the vegetable market) and 900 Decatur Street (the Halle des Boucheries-public meat market), both constructed in 1813.Under the WPA, the market buildings were extensively renovated in the 1930s, at which time the colonnade around 900 Decatur was added. The complex was again renovated in the 1970s by the city of New Orleans.

Housing a variety of shops and restaurants, this complex of buildings remains a vital part of the Quarter, from Café Du Monde on the western edge at Jackson Square to the open vegetable market-flea market on Barracks Street adjacent to the U.S. Mint.

NICHOLAS GIROD HOUSE

The Napoleon House
500 Chartres Street
Circa 1814
National Historic Landmark

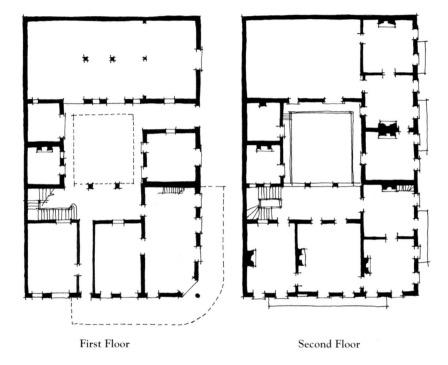

First Floor   Second Floor

The residence of Mayor Nicholas Girod, built in 1814 at the corner of Chartres and St. Louis Streets, is an excellent example of the continuing French influence in postcolonial New Orleans and was most likely designed by Hyacinthe Laclotte. The two-story wing facing St. Louis Street was built earlier, around 1797, by Nicholas's brother, Claude Francois Girod, who served as mayor of New Orleans from 1812 to 1815.

The building commonly known as the "Napoleon House" derives its name from the legend that Mayor Girod planned to engage a crew of pirates to sail secretly to the island prison and rescue Napoleon. The Napoleon House is supposedly the mansion built by Mayor Girod for the rescued emperor. Legend continues that on the day the plans were finalized and the ship was set to sail, word reached New Orleans that Napoleon had died.

The more likely story is that when the news arrived to New Orleans that Napoleon had escaped from Elba, a large group of excited locals gathered at the Cabildo. They felt that Napoleon would seek refuge in America and that New Orleans would most likely be his port of entry. Mayor Girod allegedly made a speech in which he promised that if Napoleon would come to New Orleans, he would place his own residence at the disposal of the famous exile.

Around 1914, Joseph Impastato and his wife opened a grocery in the building. The grocery expanded to sell sandwiches and house a small bar where Impastato played classical music on his Victrola, a tradition that remains to this day. Since 1980, the bar has been operated by Mr. Impastato's son, Sal.

COTTIN HOUSE

534 Royal Street
Circa 1816

The Cottin House was built for Jean Baptiste Cottin sometime between 1813, when he bought the lot, and 1818, when the property with the building on it was sold by his estate to architects-builders Gurlie and Guillot, who were most likely the designers of the building. Author Lyle Saxon lived in the house from 1920 to 1924 (Toledano 1996).

The two-story entresol townhouse features three arched openings at the first level and four openings at the second level that open onto a narrow balcony with a wrought-iron railing. The second level is embellished with Ionic pilasters at the corners and a simple, classically inspired cornice at the roofline. A carriageway leads to a rear courtyard.

Lloyd Vogt

GARNIER HOUSE

Pat O'Brien's
718 St. Peter Street
1817

Built in 1817, this house, locally known as Pat O'Brien's, was constructed for John Garnier, a planter, commission merchant, and owner of a brick kiln. The building remained in the Garnier family until 1891, when it was sold by his heirs to Mrs. Marianne Aubian Dours.

The two-story stuccoed building is a good example of the continuation of colonial forms into the American era. It has seven equally spaced French doors opening onto a wrought-iron balcony at the second level and six doors with an asymmetrically placed porte cochère at the ground level. The carriageway leads to a large rear courtyard formed by a garçonnière to one side. The courtyard facade features four paneled casement windows, topped with a fanlight transom.

In the early 1930s, a young Pat O'Brien, traveling home to Birmingham, Alabama from Los Angeles, stopped to spend a few days in New Orleans. A few days turned into weeks, months, then years, and in 1933, he leased a tiny alcove with a patio at 638 St. Peter Street for $9 a month and opened a bar. The bar became the favorite watering hole for the Quarter intellectuals, writers, artists and assorted bohemians. By 1938, its popularity had outgrown its location, and O'Brien found the building at 718 St. Peter. Four years later, and after extensive renovation, the new Pat O'Brien's opened for business and has never stopped.

Its popularity is international, and its signature drink, with an accompanying uniquely shaped glass, "the Hurricane," has sold millions. It has been said that Pat O'Brien's sells more alcohol per year than any bar in America.

FANCHON HOUSE

Preservation Hall
726 St. Peter
1817

Commonly known as Preservation Hall, 726 St. Peter Street was constructed in 1817 by Claude Gurlie and Joseph Guillot on a lot where a tavern was destroyed by fire the previous year. The house was purchased from Gurlie and Guillot the same year it was constructed by Agathe Fanchon, a free woman of color. Madame Fanchon owned the property until 1866.

The two-story, stuccoed porte cochère townhouse has three bays with two French doors and a porte cochère on the ground level, and three French doors opening onto a narrow wrought-iron balcony at the upper level. The French doors are protected by heavy vertical board shutters. The porte cochère leads to a rear courtyard with an outbuilding located to one side. The house originally had a flat roof in the Spanish tradition, but like so many others of the period, the roof was replaced by a more watertight, pitched (sloped) roof.

Through the years, the house has changed hands many times. In 1961, a group of citizens interested in preservation of traditional New Orleans music opened the house as a music club. Soon there-after, while living in the rear outbuildings, Allan and Sandra Jaffe took over the operation, making up the financial losses of the first eighteen months of operation from their own savings. Eventually, the hall gained popularity and remains popular today, having pro-vided the venue for hundreds of musicians playing to preserve the traditional music of the city.

Lloyd vogt

THE ERA OF TRANSITION: 1820-1835

THE PERIOD BETWEEN 1820 AND 1835 was a period of transition for the French Quarter, as American influence continued to gain momentum. Port trade was increasing and the economy expanding. The population grew from about 18,000 in 1812 to 30,000 in 1830 to more than 100,000 by 1840, an increase of more than 80,000 in a mere twenty-eight years.

As the Americans flooded into the city, they carried with them their architectural ideals, common on the eastern seaboard at the time and strongly influenced by English tradition. In 1807, Benjamin Latrobe (from Philadelphia) designed the custom house with exposed red brick, freestone columns, white trim, double-hung windows, and green shutters. In 1816, Henry S. Latrobe, Benjamin's son, designed a house for William Kenner, for which he specified that "the windows shall be hung with weights in the American style." Soon thereafter, double-hung windows rapidly began to replace the casement windows commonly used by the Creoles.

As the city grew and prospered, the celebration of food expanded. While most dining was done in the home, by the early 1800s, restaurant dining was rapidly gaining in popularity. Creole men frequented cafes and bars for coffee, liquor, and food while conducting business, arguing politics, or just discussing the popular topics of the day. The city represented great opportunities for becoming wealthy, and the pace of living was increasing rapidly. Leisure time was decreasing and greater energy was thrown toward the business of making money. By this time, the city had become host to three societies: the French, the American, and the mixed. However, before long, these societies would blend into a New Orleans culture.

The hustle and bustle of the street scene was infused with the Native Americans who, by historical accounts of the locals, were considered dirty and disgusting in their appearance. In the mornings Indian men could be seen scantily clothed, carrying a rifle, and having strings of birds, squirrels, raccoons, opossums, and ducks for sale to merchants or anyone on the streets. Often they could be seen painted, wrapped up in blankets, with feathers in their hair. The women wore strings of beads and brass wire rings about their arms. Some carried children on their backs. While the Native Americans' overall appearance was considered distasteful, they were considered to be scrupulously honest, and their women most scrupulously chaste.

Along with the growth and prosperity came hardships. It was during this time that the city began to experience catastrophic epidemics. In his memoirs, Reverend Theodore Clapp, for thirty-five years a Presbyterian minister in New Orleans, relates the horrors of the time:

"On the morning of the 25th of October, 1832, as I was walking home from market, before sunrise, I saw two men lying on the levee in a dying condition. They had been landed from a steamboat which arrived the night before. At first there was quite a crowd assembled on the spot. But an eminent physician rode up in his gig, and gazing a monemt, exclaimed in a loud voice, "Those men have the Asiatic cholera." The crown dispersed in a moment, and ran as if for their lives in every direction. I was left almost alone with the sufferers. They could speak, and were in full possession of their reason. They had what I afterwards found were the usual symptoms of cholera—cramps, convulsions, &c. The hands and the feet were cold and blue; an icy perspiration flowed in streams; and they complained of a great pressure upon their chests. One of them said it seemed as if a bar of iron was lying across him. Their thirst was intense, which caused an insufferable agony in the mouth and throat.

On the evening of the 27th of October, it had made its way through every part of the city. During the ten succeeding days, reckoning from October 27 to the 6th of November, all the physicians judged that, at the lowest computation, there were five thousand deaths—an average of five hundred every day. Many died of whom no account was rendered. A great number of bodies, with bricks and stones tied to the feet, were thown into the river. Many were privately interred in gardens and enclosures, on the grounds where they expired, whose names were not recorded in the bills of mortality.

The morning after (October 29), at six o'clock, I stepped into a carriage to accompany a funeral procession to the cemetery. On my arrival, I found at the graveyard a large pile of corpses without coffins, in horizontal layers, one above the other, like corded wood . . . Large trenches were dug, into which these uncoffined corpses were thrown indiscriminately. The same day, a private hospital was found deserted; the physicians, nursers, and attendants were all dead, or had run away. Not a living person was in it. The wards were filled with putrid bodies, which, by order of the mayor, were piled in an adjacent yard, and burned, and their ashes scattered to the winds.

Many persons, even of fortune and popularity, died in their beds without aid, unnoticed and unknown, and lay there for days unburied. In almost every house might be seen the sick, the dying, and the dead, in the same room. All the stores, banks, and places of business were closed. Multitudes began the day in apparently good health, and were corpses before sunset."

The waterworks, earlier developed by Benjamin Latrobe, were now operational as described by his son, John B. Latrobe, in 1834: "The water works erected by my father are in operation, and at the corners of the cross streets along the Rue de la Levee, I saw this morning the water bubbling up from the pipes into the large cast iron box around them, and running off in a rapid stream through the gutters. At every corner were crowds of negro women filling their buckets and water carts supplying themselves from a less defiled place than the margin of the river."

The riverfront was a hotbed of activity, teeming with seamen from a dozen nations, the American river men, and countless slaves. Moored to heavy timbers embedded in the *batture* were boats from Europe, the eastern seaboard ports of New England, New York, Baltimore, and Philadelphia, and various ports from the Caribbean Islands. In addition, the port moored a dozen or more Mississippi River steamboats, the newest in American nautical navigation. From Europe and New England came cotton, liquors, coffee, spices, farming implements, wool, furniture, and iron billets for the foundries. From upriver came hemp, tobacco, flour, sugar, the first bales of cotton, and shipments of furs destined for the markets of Europe.

The tremendous wealth generated during this era created a distinct luxury class. The young men from prominent Creole families were sent to Europe to be educated—most frequently to Paris. Upon returning to New Orleans, they had money and plenty of leisure

113

time, a combination which resulted in an era of confrontation. In this time of honor, when etiquette and politeness were of utmost importance to the young aristocratic Creoles, dueling reached its extreme, becoming so popular that fencing academies created great wealth for many fencing masters. These masters formed a social class of their own and became the envy of the city's privileged youth.

Mardi Gras celebrations in New Orleans are almost as old as the city itself, with carnival balls held every season, but by the 1820s, these celebrations began to evolve into the form that we know today. Parades, consisting of bands of masquers parading through the streets and throwing confetti and flour on onlookers, began in the 1820s and continued for three decades. The first parade using vehicles took place in 1839—an assortment of wagons and carriages winding through the streets, terminating with an evening ball. The first carnival organization, the Mistick Krewe of Comus, was founded in 1857 and held its first parade that same year. Thereafter, Mardi Gras continued to expand year after year, evolving into the immense festival it has become today.

114

BUILDING TYPES & STYLES

The majority of houses constructed during this period were of two types: American Creole cottages and American townhouses. Research indicates that the shotgun house was introduced to America through the port of New Orleans during this time, and although never achieving the popularity of Creole cottages and townhouses in the Quarter, it spread to other areas of the city and to communities throughout the South.

Until about 1820, the predominant architectural style in the Quarter remained essentially Creole. Houses were generally painted yellow with white pilasters on the corners and white facings on all the openings. From about 1820 to 1835, there was a gradual transition to an American architecture, affecting building types, styles, materials, and ornaments. Once introduced, exposed, red-brick facades rapidly gained popularity and were so well received that even the prominent Creole architects began to design in this fashion. Locally made bricks proved to be too porous when left exposed to the New Orleans climate, and consequently, many houses constructed of local brick were later stuccoed over or painted to combat the moisture problems—lessons learned a hundred years earlier and obviously forgotten. To achieve the desired effect, brick houses were frequently painted a brick-red color with joints "penciled in" with white paint. Before long, much of the brick being used in an exposed manner was imported from Baltimore and Philadelphia, bricks less porous and better suited for exposure to the climate. Classical forms took on a more delicate character than previously exhibited—narrow, flat pilasters and delicate, richly ornamented stuccoed cornices became common on the upper story of many new buildings.

The American Creole Cottage

Creole cottages remained popular, but many were now constructed with exposed red brick and double-hung windows, in lieu of stucco finishes, and casement windows and main entrances exhibited classical detailing.

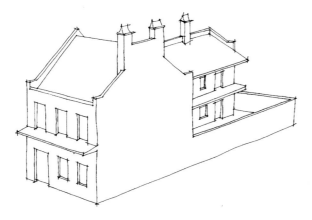

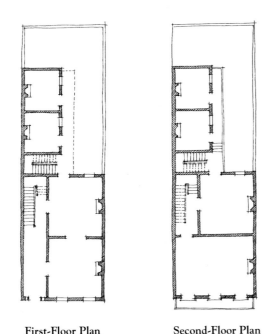

First-Floor Plan   Second-Floor Plan

The American Townhouse

The American townhouse gradually replaced the Creole townhouse in popularity. The basic form and layout was similar to its Creole predecessor, with a service wing projecting into the rear courtyard. The major differences, however, were the introduction of a highly detailed entrance in the classical manner, the absence of a carriageway, and the use of halls in the interior of the house.

Row houses (attached townhouses) were now being built and were similar to those popular in eastern seaboard cities such as Boston, Baltimore, and Philadelphia. Primarily of English influence, they varied in number from as few as two or three to as many as fourteen. Most commonly two or three stories in height, some four-story row houses were also constructed.

Constructed of red brick, America townhouses were approximately thirty feet wide and had three openings on the front facade at each level. The ground-floor facade generally had a classically detailed entrance to one side, with double-hung windows protected by louvered or vertical plank shutters. A balcony with a wrought-iron railing ran across the entire facade at the second level, accessed through French doors with decorative transoms or through full-length double-hung windows. The classical entrance, windows, and cornices at the roofline were painted white and shutters green, in contrast to the exposed red brick. Gabled roofs, covered with slate shingles pitched to the front and rear, were similar to Creole townhouses and frequently had dormers illuminating the attic. Brick chimneys extended upward from the side, brick, fire walls in rabbit-ears fashion.

Shotgun Houses

The defining characteristic of a shotgun house is the location of the entry on the narrow side of the house, in contrast to the typical European tradition of entry on the long side. The shotgun house is a simple rectangular building, one room wide, three or more rooms deep, with no halls, and with all of the rooms arranged directly behind one another in a straight line. The door to each room is normally located on the same side, so that all of the doors are aligned. The term "shotgun" is said to have originated from the notion that if a shotgun were fired through the front door, all the pellets would exit the rear door unobstructed.

Research suggests that the shotgun house evolved in Haiti, from a blending of African and Haitian-Indian house forms, and was introduced into New Orleans in the early 1800s at about the time the city experienced an influx of free Negroes fleeing the revolutions in Haiti. Historical links between Haiti and Louisiana—fused by French culture, trade, and commerce—reinforces this probability.

In the early days of French colonization, a large number of slaves were brought to Haiti, where they preserved many of their native cultural traditions. A large number of these slaves were from Yoruba land, West African. John Michael Vlach noted: "My field work shows that the basic Yoruba house form is a ten foot by twenty foot two-room building and is used by both the Yoruba and their Edo neighbors to the southeast."

The house form that the slaves introduced into Haiti was very similar to that of the native Arawak Indians and the shotgun house most likely evolved as a blending of Yoruba and Arawak characteristics, as the dwellings for the slaves were constructed on sugarcane plantations. As a result, southern Haiti has many shotgun houses very similar to those in New Orleans. The shotguns of Port-au-Prince are similar not only in type but also in detail—room height, width, and length are very compatible (Vlach 1975)

While research suggests the Haitian connection, an illustrative map of the Spanish colonial city of Panama City, Panama clearly indicates almost all of the houses are one room wide and entered from the short side. One more example of the difficulty of clearly establishing origins of the architecture that evolved from the greater Caribbean, Gulf of Mexico basin. In addition, recent local research challenges the date of introduction of the shotgun house into the city, indicating that the type was not built in New Orleans until the 1840s. Further research will be needed to resolve this ongoing controversy.

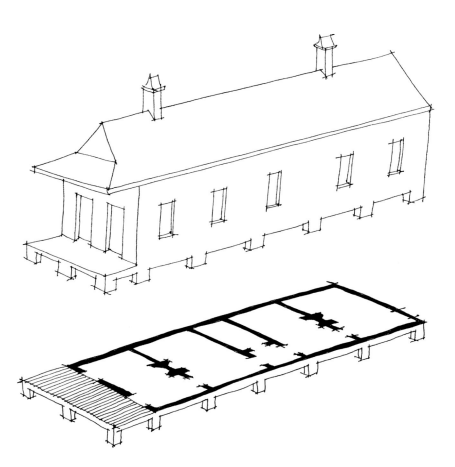

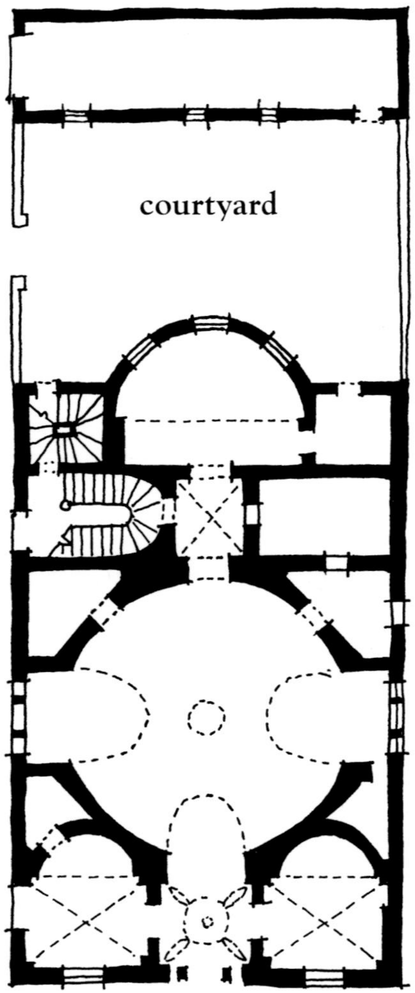

LOUISIANA STATE BANK

403 Royal Street
1820
National Historic Landmark

The Louisiana State Bank was designed in 1820 by Benjamin Henry Latrobe shortly before his death from yellow fever. The builder was Benjamin Fowler Fox. Latrobe was the architect of the capital in Washington D.C. and the Baltimore Cathedral before coming to New Orleans in 1819 to oversee the development of the New Orleans waterworks system.

The ground-floor vaulting and dome of the bank are of brick masonry and the plan is reminiscent of the Bank of Pennsylvania in Philadelphia, Latrobe's first great American work after his arrival from his native England.

The building originally had an almost flat-tile terrace roof, now covered by a hip roof. The curved wall facing the rear courtyard enclosed the director's room on the ground floor and the dining room in the cashier's apartment on the second floor.

courtyard

LE CARPENTIER/
BEAUREGARD-KEYES HOUSE

1113 Chartres Street
1826
National Historic Landmark

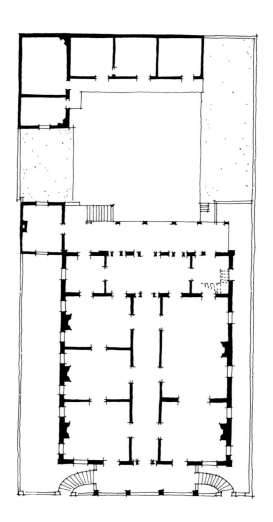

Located opposite the Ursuline Convent, the residence of the late novelist Frances Parkinson Keyes is owned by the Keyes Foundation, founded by Mrs. Keyes to assure the preservation of the house and gardens.

In 1826 Joseph Le Carpentier obtained plans for the house designed by Francois Correjolles, one of the first native-born Americans (Baltimore) to achieve success as an architect in New Orleans. His work reflects the American influence on local Creole architecture. The contractor for the residence was James Lambert.

Paul Morphy, Le Carpentier's grandson who became America's chess master, was born at the residence in 1837. The house was also the site of the slaying of three members of the Sicilian Mafia, allegedly by Pietro Giacona and his son Corrado in retaliation for an extortion attempt against their wine business. The slaying was said to be one of the most dramatic of the long list of Italian "Black Hand" feuds in the city's history. The Giaconas were indicted for murder but were never convicted. The case was eventually dropped.

The house has also been used as a meeting hall for civic groups, and it was here, in 1931, that the La Renaissance du Vieux Carré, one of the earliest preservation organizations in the city, was formed—there mission, to promote and encourage preservation and restoration. Approximately twenty years later, the Louisiana Landmarks Society was founded, appropriately, in the same house.

MORTUARY CHAPEL

Our Lady of Guadeloupe Catholic Church
411 North Rampart Street
1826-27

The oldest church building in New Orleans, the Mortuary Chapel of Saint Anthony of Padua was built in 1826, after funerals were forbidden by city ordinance at St. Louis Cathedral because of yellow fever epidemics. It was designed and constructed by Claude Gurlie and Joseph Guillot, architects. Although not technically within the boundary of the Quarter, the chapel is an integral part of the Quarter's history.

In 1918, under the charge of the Oblate Fathers of Mary Immaculate, it was renamed Our Lady of Guadeloupe Catholic Church. In 1924, the grotto to Our Lady of Lourdes was built, and in 1935, the first public novena in honor of Saint Jude was celebrated. In 1931, it became the chapel of the New Orleans police and fire departments. It was enlarged and remodeled in 1952. Today, the church is home to the International Shrine of Saint Jude.

Lloyd Vogt

BANK OF LOUISIANA

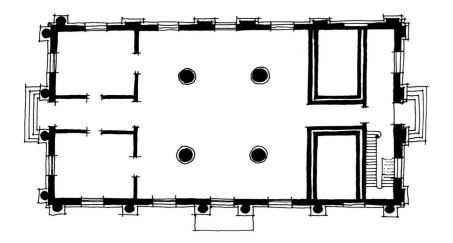

The Old Mortgage Office
334 Royal Street
1826
National Historic Landmark

The Bank of Louisiana was designed by Benjamin F. Fox and constructed in 1826, at a cost of $80,000, by Bickle, Hamblet, and Fox, builders. The site was purchased in 1825 by the Bank of Louisiana from the heirs of Jean Noel Destrehan. At the time of construction, the corner of Royal and Conti streets was the hub of the city's financial activities, three of the four corners having a bank. It was the second institution to be known as the Bank of Louisiana and served as the city's financial center for many years. The bank closed during the Civil War.

The building was damaged by fire in 1840, 1861, and 1931. Renovations to the building, which included the classical portico on the Royal Street entrance, were made by architect James Gallier, Jr. After the bank's closing in 1867, the building provided housing for numerous occupants: Louisiana State Capital, an auction exchange, a saloon, a courthouse, and the American Legion (who used the building for almost fifty years).

The iron gates at the entrance are a facsimile of the garden entrance of the Lansdowne House in Berkeley Square, London, designed for the marquis of Lansdowne in 1765.

The city purchased the building in 1874 and has retained ownership since that time. Since 1992, it has served as office for the Vieux Carré Commission and the Vieux Carré District police.

Lloyd Vogt

HERMANN-GRIMA HOUSE

820 Saint Louis Street
1831
National Historic Landmark

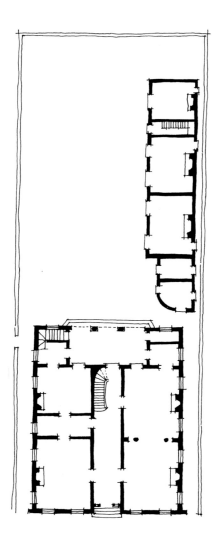

The Hermann-Grima House is one of the best examples of American influence on the architecture of the French Quarter. It was constructed by William Brand in 1831 for Samuel Hermann, Sr. (a wealthy German-Jewish merchant), and his Creole bride. In 1837, Hermann experienced a major financial setback. To settle his debts, he sold the property in 1844 to the Creole family of Felix Grima, a prominent New Orleans judge. In 1850 Grima expanded the property by purchasing the land adjacent to the residence as a site for a stable. Five generations of Grimas lived in the house before it was sold in 1921. During the Civil War, the building served as quarters for Union officers during their occupation of New Orleans

In 1924, the house was sold to the Christian Women's Exchange, the oldest chartered women's organization in New Orleans, whose mission was to provide needy women the means to earn a living. After being used as a shop and rooming house, it was opened to the public for tours as a museum house in 1965, and in 1973, it was restored under the direction of architect and historian Samuel Wilson, Jr.

The house is constructed of brick imported from Philadelphia and laid in a Flemish bond. In the rear of the house is a secluded courtyard with a three-story outbuilding, separate kitchen, and stable on the adjacent property. Unusual by Quarter standards, the house is raised slightly above grade and features a central entrance detailed in the Georgian manner, a good example of the emerging American influence upon the Quarter.

Lloyd Vogt

TRICOU HOUSE

711 Bourbon Street
1834

The Tricou House was built in 1834 by Joseph Adolphe Tricou soon after he purchased the site from Alexander Barron. The architects-builders were Claude Gurlie and Joseph Guillot. Unfortunately, Mr. Tricou only enjoyed the house for a very short period of time: he died in 1835. In that same year, the house was sold to Julien Seghers, a wealthy St. Charles Parish planter.

In 1925, under the direction of Armstrong and Koch, the house was restored by Mr. and Mrs. Charles Wogan, on of the first to be restored as the Quarter was being rediscovered and appreciated after a long period of neglect.

The first floor of the street facade features a central porte cochère flanked by two arched openings with French doors (currently removed) on each side. The second floor has a central door flanked by double-hung windows with a panel below. The wide cornice at the roofline is embellished with heavy wooden paneled doors, a swag motif, a typical feature of Gurlie and Guillot's work, and is similar to a number of other French Quarter houses executed by the pair. The wrought-iron balcony with its *garde de frise* is also typical of the period.

THE ANTEBELLUM ERA 1835—1861

THE GOLDEN ERA OF NEW ORLEANS was the antebellum era. Sailing ships from all over the world and glamorous riverboats frequented the port, and wealthy cotton and sugarcane planters with nearby plantations built exquisite mansions as their townhomes. America, still in its youth, was searching for identity and the accomplishments of classical Greece provided a source of inspiration. The Greek tradition symbolized liberty, and once introduced, the Greek Revival style spread throughout the country.

Immigrants continued to arrive in New Orleans and construction was booming. The city had fine restaurants, an opera, and grand hotels and hosted lavish balls, banquets, and parades. Gambling and dueling were common, as was the practice of voodoo. The city was an action-filled melting pot. Although New Orleans was the wealthiest city in the United States, the miseries of poverty coexisted with the prosperity. Much of the city was filthy, and its many unpaved streets were frequently flooded by heavy rains—its sewers were open drains. Typhoid, cholera, malaria, and yellow fever were ever-present threats, as the city struggled through twelve devastating epidemics in thirty-five years. Most New Orleanians obtained their drinking water from rear-yard cisterns, which, although not realized at the time, were the breeding grounds for the *Aedes aegypti* mosquito, carrier of deadly yellow fever; and coupled with the fact that the city was surrounded by swamps (another excellent breeding ground), the dreaded disease was a constant threat.

The Americans proved to be very successful businessmen, and, as their numbers increased, so did their economic base and political force. They concentrated their development above Canal Street, in Faubourg St. Mary, while the Creoles kept control of the French Quarter. The two cultures remained at odds and the city council, with a Creole majority, continually prevented public improvement projects (such as street paving and dock improvements) in the American sector.

However, by 1835, the struggle for economic control of the city began to shift in favor of the Americans. They succeeded in having the state legislature create three separate municipalities: the Vieux Carré, Faubourg St. Mary, and Faubourg Marigny (downriver from the Vieux Carré)—a division that lasted for eighteen years. In 1853 the city was once again united.

The earliest railroad in New Orleans (with horse-drawn cars) was chartered in 1830 and ran from Elysian Fields, on the downriver edge of the Quarter, to Lake Pontchartrain. Two years later, the first steam locomotive was introduced, and the system expanded rapidly, eventually servicing the entire city.

New Orleans continued to grow, and by 1840 (the year Antoine's Restaurant was opened on St. Louis Street), with a population of over 100,000, it surpassed Philadelphia and Boston to become the third-largest city in the United States, behind only New York and Baltimore. The streets of the Quarter were now being lit by lanterns suspended on ropes—gas lanterns on major streets and oil lanterns on secondary streets. Cotton presses were constructed on the riverfront and became a vital aspect of the port economy. Cotton (the chief crop of the nearby plantations) was being shipped on steamboats and the port was thriving. Soon, it was the second-most-active port in America—only New York was larger.

In 1853, New Orleans experienced the worst yellow-fever epidemic in its history, taking the lives of over 10,000 people—the death rate in New Orleans was twice that of most other urban areas in America. However, while living through these perils, there was Mardi Gras, a regular opera season, concerts, and horse racing, and the Africans spent their Sunday afternoons dancing at Congo Square. Although the celebration of Mardi Gras had been brought to Louisiana by Iberville and Bienville with the christening of Mardi Gras Bayou, in 1699, it had not played a major role in the city. In 1837, the first parade was held, and in 1839, the first float in a parade made its appearance. In 1857, the Mistick Krewe of Comus was founded, creating the Mardi Gras tradition as we know it today.

In the Quarter excessive drinking was widespread, prostitution was legal, gambling was a way of life, and political corruption and illegal voting was tolerated. Royal Street was lined with gambling houses, where Creole planters matched their skill against professional gamblers and Americans who had recently arrived. Mardi Gras festivities were growing more lavish every year; balls were held every night.

While epidemics continued to plague the city, claiming the lives of thousands, it was nevertheless an era of continual growth. The years following the worst plagues found Mardi Gras festivities more festive than ever. No one was preoccupied with the future; every one, it seems, made the most of the present (Saxon 1988).

Meanwhile, in architecture, Americans were beginning to question the basis of the classical tradition that they had so fervently embraced for fifty years. A growing protest surfaced as America began to search for a new style of expression. A newfound confidence and growing self-esteem gradually eroded adherence to the concepts of the Greek Revival, paving the way for the romantic era.

By 1860, the population of New Orleans had grown to approximately 170,000, an increase of 150,000 in a short period of fifty years. It was now the largest city in the South and the largest cotton market in the world. Thirty-five hundred steamboats docked at its wharfs and its trade totaled over $300 million, with wharf tonnage double that of New York City. Louisiana's per-capita wealth was second only to Connecticut's and the city was an international melting pot, with forty-one percent of its residents being foreign-born, representing thirty-two nations.

The prosperity, however, would soon come to an end, as the conflict between the North and the South escalated and the inevitability of war became a reality.

BUILDING TYPES

The American townhouse (as previously described) became the standard house for the newcomers and was very similar to those being constructed in New York, Philadelphia, and Baltimore. However, in New Orleans, in response to the subtropical climate, they were built with higher ceilings than their Northern counterparts.

The Greek Revival style also extended to the Creole cottages (as described earlier), which were now being constructed with red brick, white doors and windows, green shutters, and classical detailing.

L. VOGT

131

BUILDING STYLES

Greek Revival dominated the style of architecture in the Quarter during this era.

Greek Revival Style

Drawing its inspiration from the architecture of ancient Greece, the Greek Revival in America was launched in 1818 with the design of the Second Bank of Philadelphia by William Strickland, a former pupil of British architect Benjamin Henry Latrobe. New York architect Menard Lefever popularized the style through the publication of three books: *The Young Builder's General Instructor* (1829), *The Modern Builders' Guide* (1833), and *The Beauties of Modern Architecture* (1835).

Influenced by the influx of Americans into the city, the Greek Revival style began to appear in New Orleans about 1830. It was the fourth phase in the evolution of classical-revival architecture in America, after Georgian, Federal, and Jeffersonian classicism. Since New Orleans was a French and Spanish colony unaffected by the architecture favored in the English colonies, Greek Revival was the first of the classical-revival styles to gain popularity in the city.

In 1835, two New Yorkers, James Gallier and Charles B. Dakin, arrived in New Orleans, established an architectural practice, and began to spread the philosophy and popularity of the Greek Revival style. The American townhouse (which replaced the popular Creole townhouse) was the most common building type constructed in this style. Built at the sidewalk, two, three, or four stories in height, the classicism of the townhouses was manifest by detailing rather than classical temple forms. Red-brick facades, white trim, and green shutters became the norm. Entrances were prominently featured in a classical manner. Entrance doors were paneled, frequently flanked by sidelights and a rectangular transom, and framed with classical pilasters and cornices. Window surrounds were simply detailed, and shutters were most often the operable-louver type. Door and window openings were always flat-topped. Another distinguishing characteristic was the Greek-key entrance doorway (also known as crossettes), characterized by a slightly overlapping lintel and a slight flaring-out of the face of the surround from the top to the bottom.

Although not common, the Greek-temple form was occasionally utilized, such as with the Beauregard-Keyes House and the United States Mint. Also during this time, gray, granite, classically detailed pillars were introduced on ground-level street facades in order to provide more windows for ground-floor shops and to allow natural light to reach deeper into the interior of buildings. In addition to new construction, many buildings previously constructed with arched brick openings were now modernized by replacing the arches with granite pillars.

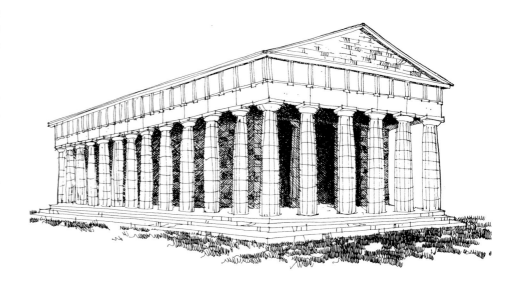

Greek temple, Athens, c. 430 B.C.

132

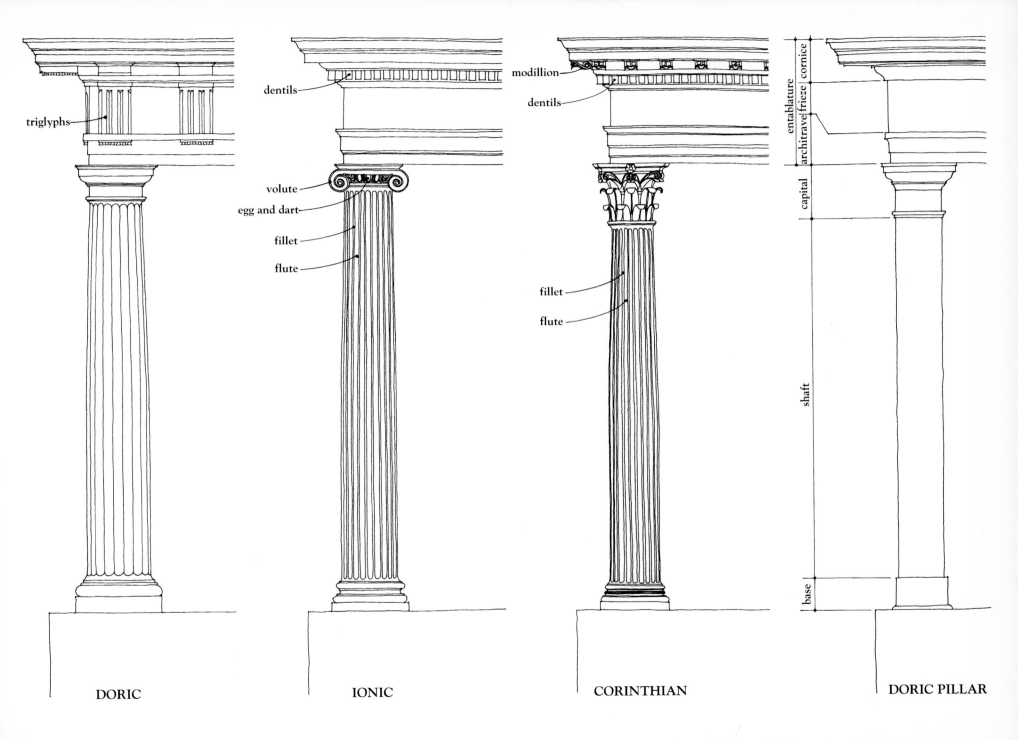

triglyphs

dentils

volute

egg and dart

fillet

flute

modillion

dentils

fillet

flute

entablature
cornice
frieze
architrave

capital

shaft

base

DORIC

IONIC

CORINTHIAN

DORIC PILLAR

CAST IRON:
FROM BALCONIES TO GALLERIES

The technique for processing iron was discovered as early as 1500 B.C. in Asia Minor; however, the capacity to heat iron so that it could be cast into shapes was developed in China between 600 and 500 B.C. Wrought iron is distinguished from cast iron by its carbon content. It contains less carbon than cast iron, making it malleable and allowing it to be shaped by hammering, stretching, or rolling, while cast iron, with a higher carbon content, is brittle and fractures easily upon impact. In making cast iron, the raw material is melted in a furnace and the molten iron is poured into a prepared mold. After cooling and finishing, the product is ready for use.

Margot and Carol Gayle tell us: "Britain, with its advantageous combination of seams of iron ore near the surface and sufficient timber from which to make charcoal, became a significant producer of cast iron from the fifteenth century. But it was in the seventeenth century that "the cast iron industry really began to be established."

The use of cast iron in America lagged behind that of Britain and France, primarily because in eighteenth-century America, there were few cities of size. The rapid growth of America in the first half of the nineteenth century, however, greatly stimulated the iron industry. Although greatly influenced by English technology, companies in New York, Philadelphia, and Baltimore quickly became the industry leaders. Cast iron's first use in America appears in the 1820s; by the 1830s, cast-iron columns were being used for framing in factories, and by 1840, its use had extended for slender columns in shop-front display windows (Gayle 1998). The cast-iron industry in New Orleans began with the establishment of the Leeds Iron Foundry in 1825. By the 1830s, cast iron was being used in combination with wrought iron.

The extensive use of cast iron as an architectural element in New Orleans was most likely introduced in 1849, with the construction of the Pontalba buildings flanking Jackson Square. Designed by James Gallier and later modified by Henry Howard, the buildings utilized cast iron on their street-front galleries. While the cast iron used on the Pontalba buildings was manufactured in New York, and many others in the Quarter undoubtedly imported from the large foundries in Philadelphia and New York, most of the iron used in New Orleans was probably cast locally. Local foundries produced railings, columns, and capitals, and in some cases, entire cast-iron facades.

Cast iron is suitable for many designs, especially the complex naturalistic patterns popular with the Victorians. The variety of railing patterns available during the nineteenth century was extensive and trade catalogs advertising standardized items were produced by the more successful firms. This played an instrumental role in spreading the popularity of ironwork.

The growing popularity of cast iron helped facilitate the evolution of one of the Quarter's most distinguishing characteristics. Most of the early buildings in the Quarter had small cantilevered balconies on the upper levels, similar to those found in Europe and the islands of the West Indies. However, in New Orleans these balconies afforded little protection from the torrential rains and torrid summer sun, and eventually, a solution evolved. The balconies at the first level of two- and three-story buildings were extended to the edge of the sidewalk. First supported by cypress posts, they were soon replaced with iron colonnettes.

As the popularity of the idea grew, new buildings featured galleries extending up two and three stories, covering entire facades in a delicate lacework of iron. In many instances, cast-iron columns, galleries, balconies, and railings were added to existing structures, substantially changing their appearance, and consequently, the character of the entire Quarter. The extensive use of cast iron for multistory galleries has given the Quarter a character that is unique, and, coupled with courtyards accessed by porte cochères, has become its defining characteristic. With possibly the exception of Sydney and Melbourne, Australia, the French Quarter houses the world's greatest collection of ornamental cast iron.

GARDETTE-LE PRETRE HOUSE

716 Dauphine Street
1836

This imposing building located at the corner of Dauphine and Orleans streets was constructed in 1836 by Fredrick Roy for Dr. Joseph Coulon Gardette, a dentist. Dr. Gardette sold the building in 1839 to Jean Baptiste Le Prêtre, a well-known merchant and banker, and it became a prominent center of social activity during his residency. The house is an imposing townhouse wrapped in a delicate lace of cast-iron galleries, supported at the first level by columns eighteen feet tall. The cast-iron galleries were added sometime after 1850.

In 1869, the building was taken over by the Citizens' Bank and converted for commercial use. Eventually, the building began to deteriorate and an early preservationist, Mrs. Philip Werlein, saved the house from demolition. In 1959, Mrs. Robert L. Hines bought the property and sensitively restored it.

UNITED STATES MINT

400 Esplanade Avenue
1838
National Historic Landmark

Located on Esplanade Avenue near the riverfront (on the original site of Fort San Carlos, erected in 1792 by Spanish governor François Louis Hector, Baron de Carondelet) the United States Mint was erected in 1838 by John Mitchell and Benjamin F. Fox, following the designs of William Strickland. The mint operated until 1909.

During the Civil War, the building was seized by the Confederacy and was used for minting Confederate coins for a brief period. It was transferred to the State of Louisiana in 1966 and was renovated to become the Louisiana State Museum in 1978-80.

The Esplanade Avenue facade of this Greek Revival building incorporates a central, classical, projecting portico featuring Ionic columns with granite capitals and bases. A pair of granite stairs running parallel to the street are hidden behind the wall at the ground level. Expansive wings flank the central temple-like portico to a width of 282 feet. The building is constructed of brick and plastered and scored, simulating stone blocks. The rear of the building creates a backdrop for the active flea market, which is part of the French Market produce facility.

The building was designated a national historic landmark in 1975.

VICTOR DAVID HOUSE

Le Petit Salon
620 Saint Peter Street
1838

Le Petit Salon was constructed by David Sidle and Samuel Stewart, of Sidle and Stewart, in 1838 for Victor David, a wealthy French hardware merchant who immigrated to America in the wake of the fall of Napoleon. His company supplied hardware for many important buildings in New Orleans and nearby plantations in the prosperous 1830s. The architect of the building is unknown.

A side-hall American townhouse constructed of brick, this four-and-a-half-story building is very unusual for the Quarter, as its main level and entry is raised a full floor above the street, reached by an exterior curved stairway. Each floor has a projecting balcony with wrought-iron railings of different designs. The third-floor balcony has a very unusual and distinctive crossed-arrow pattern.

The house remained in the David family until it was sold in 1876 by his heir, Mrs. Marie Celeste David, widow of Matthew Jules Bujac. From 1882 to 1885, the house was owned by Edward Bermudez, Chief Justice of the Louisiana Supreme Court. His heirs owned the house until 1921. In 1925, acting for Le Petit Salon, it was bought and restored by Miss Grace King, whereby it became used for meetings and receptions. Greek Revival in style, the house contains many ornamental details found in Menard Lefever's *Beauties of Modern Architecture*.

THE ARSENAL

600 Saint Peter Street
1839

Designed by James Dakin, the building located in the immediate rear of the Cabildo and opposite Le Petit Salon served as the state arsenal from 1840 until 1915. It is constructed on the site of the old Spanish prison and was first occupied by the Louisiana Legion, an aristocratic military organization of men from prestigious Creole and American families. Their monogram "LL", with two crossed cannons above a pile of cannonballs, is still evident. Massive square pilasters, framing vertical windows protected by a gridded screen of iron straps, order the front facade, and a large door with metal rivets provides entry.

During the Civil War, both Confederate and Union forces occupied the building. It was turned over to the Louisiana State Museum during the centennial of the Battle of New Orleans in 1914, when it became a museum, commemorating the bravery of Louisianians at war. Today, the museum houses relics of many wars, including the early Indian Wars, the Revolutionary War, Galvez's expedition against the British in West Florida, the War of 1812, the Battle of New Orleans, the Civil War, the Spanish-American War, and World War II.

Wood Vogt

LABRANCHE BUILDINGS

700-712 Royal Street
621-639 Saint Peter Street
622-624 Pirate's Alley
1840

Located where Royal Street meets St. Peter Street, the LaBranche buildings consist of a group of eleven three-story row houses constructed of brick for Melasie Trepagnier LaBranche, widow of Jean Baptiste LaBranche, a wealthy sugarcane planter in St. Charles Parish. On this site originally stood part of the yard of the French colonial prison.

The buildings employ extensive use of cast-iron balconies designed in a motif of entwined oak leaves and acorns. The balconies, which replaced earlier wrought-iron balconies after 1850, are acknowledged as some of the finest examples of cast iron found in the city. Along the Pirate's Alley facade, the original wrought-iron balconies can be seen.

JACKSON SQUARE

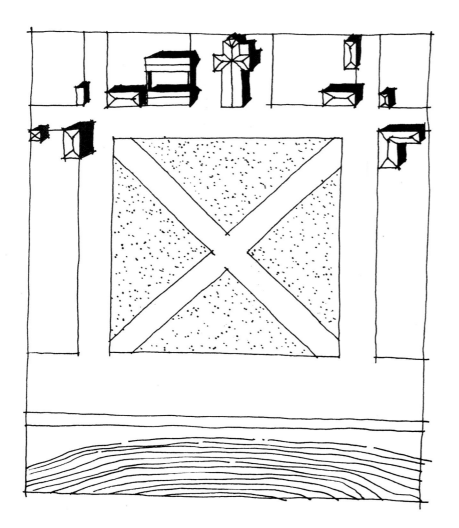

Place d'Armes (Plaza de Armas)
National Historic Landmark

Following the plan of Leblond de La Tour, Place d'Armes was laid out by Adrien de Pauger in 1721. Conceived as the center of the new colony, the square has served this function well for almost three hundred years, playing host to many of the city's major historical events. It was here, in 1769, that the French surrendered the colony to the Spanish (whereby it became Plaza de Armas), and where, in 1803, the formal transfer of the colony to the United States took place, shortly after the Louisiana Purchase.

Jackson Square, as it is today, was laid out around 1850, most likely from plans submitted by the Baroness de Pontalba, Micaela Almonester, the developer of the Pontalba buildings, which flank the Square. The cast-iron fence, designed by city surveyor Louis H. Pilié, was erected in 1851. The bronze, equestrian statue of Maj. Gen. Andrew Jackson, by sculptor Clark Mills, was erected in 1856.

From Christmas caroling to New Year's Eve celebrations, as intended, Jackson Square remains the heart of the Quarter and the entire city.

Jackson Square was designated a national historic landmark in 1960.

L. vogt

SAINT LOUIS CATHEDRAL

Jackson Square
1849-1851

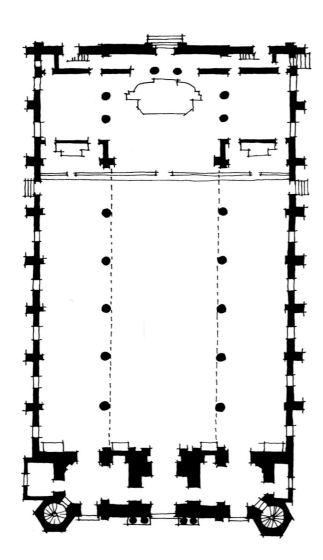

The first church in New Orleans constructed by the French colonists was built near this site soon after Bienville's founding of the city in 1718. The church was destroyed by a hurricane in 1722, and a new church, designed by Adrien de Pauger, was constructed between 1724 and 1727. The Great Fire of 1788 destroyed the new church, and a third church, financed by Don Andrés Almonester y Roxas, was designed by Gilberto Guillemard in 1794. In 1820, a central tower was built, following the plan of Benjamin H. Latrobe. After the collapse of the central tower in 1850, the church was practically demolished and replaced by the present St. Louis Cathedral, designed by the architect J. N. B. dePouilly. The cathedral includes a part of the front wall of the 1794 building.

The baroque details on the St. Louis Cathedral are similar to those in the pediment and attic story of the main building at the Ursuline Convent. DePouilly may have remodeled the convent at the same time as the cathedral.

The front facade of the cathedral is quite unique, exhibiting a combination of flanking towers, in the French-Spanish tradition, and a central tower, in the English tradition, as established with the work of Sir Christopher Wren in London. The classical revival church is ranked a minor basilica by the Catholic church.

Lloyd Vogt

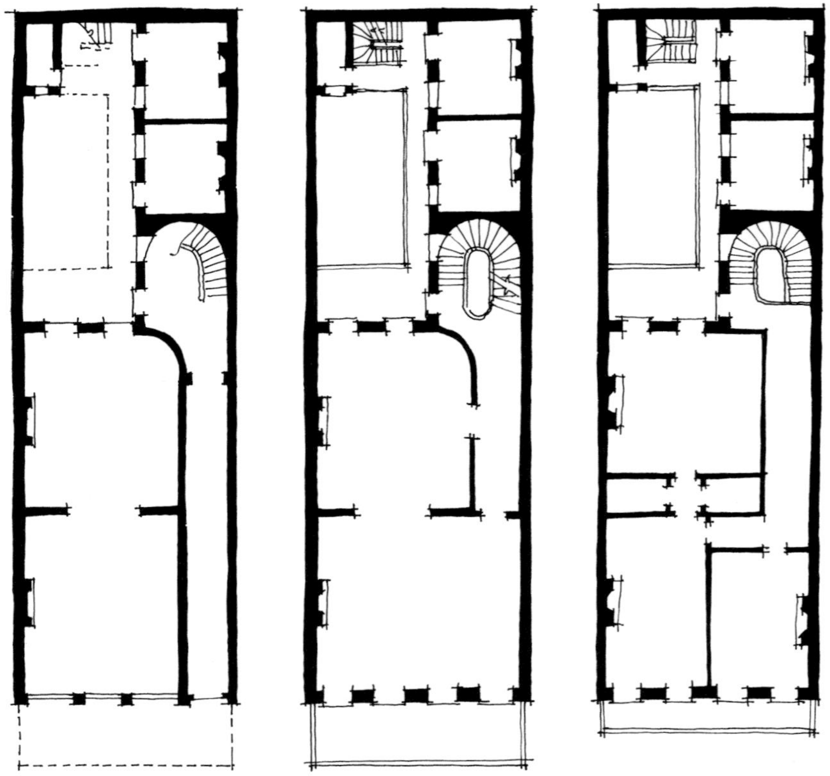

PONTALBA BUILDINGS

Jackson Square
1849
National Historic Landmark

The Pontalba buildings flanking each side of Jackson Square were built for the Baroness de Pontalba, Micaela Almonester. In 1849 she contracted with James Gallier, Sr., to design sixteen row houses to replace the deteriorating houses and shops constructed in 1768, which she had inherited from her father.

Midway in the project, Henry Howard replaced Gallier as the architect, and the baroness returned to New Orleans from Paris to oversee the construction. Cast-iron galleries were incorporated into the design, most likely the first to be used in the Quarter. In traditional Greek Revival style, the first floor utilizes heavy granite columns, with Philadelphia brick above. 1849

The desire of the baroness to renovate the center of the Quarter spilled over to Jackson Square, which she submitted plans for, and from which the renovated square, as it stands today, most likely followed.

First Floor   Second Floor   Third Floor

150

MAJOR GENERAL
ANDREW JACKSON

Lloyd Vogt

XIQUES HOUSE

521 Dauphine Street
1852

The Xiques House, designed by architect J. N. B. dePouilly for a wealthy Spaniard named Angel Xiques, was constructed circa 1852. Xiques, a native of Cadiz, Spain, was a partner in Laborde and Xiques, importers of Cuban products, including cigars, tobacco, seeds, and coffee. After the death of Xiques, the house was sold by his widow in 1867 to Dona Amalia Laborde Camba (wife of Angel Padro Garcia) and her sister, Maria Victoria Laborde Seco Fontecha, for $25,000.

Thereafter, the building hosted a number of different occupants. From 1871 to 1877, it served as the Spanish Consulate. Under the direction of Emanuel Rodrigues, the house became a gambling establishment known as the Lion. The enterprise became a disreputable "hell," which was closed by the authorities after the murder of a Spanish consul. Considering the boisterous climate of the times, it was quite a distinction to be judged too unruly to remain in business.

In 1892, the building was sold at a sheriff's auction for $39.80, the amount owed for taxes. In the 1930s, the house was a rooming house with a store at the first level.

This imposing, raised basement, Greek Revival house resembles a rural villa more than it resembles an urban townhouse, and is quite unusual for the Quarter.

Lloyd Vogt

GALLIER HOUSE

1132 Royal St
1857
National Historic Landmark

The Gallier House was designed by James Gallier, Jr., as his personal residence in 1857. A double-galleried, Greek Revival-American townhouse, it reflects the influences of both the New Orleans climate and the growing romantic movement in America. Gallier and his wife, Aglae Villavasso, lived in the house with their four daughters until he died at the age of forty-one in 1868. His widow and children continued to live in the house until 1917.

The house features many innovations of the time, such as internal plumbing. In the courtyard of the house is a cypress cistern that was moved from the Gold Mine Plantation in St. James Parish. Ten feet tall, with a metal cover rising another four feet, it sits on a round, brick base approximately eight feet in diameter and four and one-half feet high. This raised cistern provided sufficient height for providing adequate water pressure for internal plumbing.

The house now serves as a museum and is open to the public.

First-Floor Plan   Second-Floor Plan

154

GREEK REVIVAL-AMERICAN TOWNHOUSES

308, 310, 314 North Rampart Street
Circa 1840

Built as part of a complex of row houses, these three remaining American townhouses are good examples of the simple elegance of the Greek Revival style. Constructed of brick, with a stucco finish, these two- and one-half-story townhouses are typical of the type and style of the 1830s and 1840s.

Each house has three fenestrations on the front façade, two French doors with a side entrance on the first level, and French doors flanked by six-over-six, full-length windows opening onto a narrow cantilevered balcony with simple wrought-iron railings at the second level. The entranceway has a four-panel wooden door with a transom above a Greek-key surround. Board shutters protect the first-floor openings, while louvered shutters are utilized at the second level. Attic windows at the upper level merge into a denticulated cornice at the roofline.

THE VICTORIAN ERA 1861—1900

THE CIVIL WAR

LOUISIANA SECEDED FROM THE UNION in January 1861 and on March 25 joined the Confederate States of America. New Orleans was the largest and richest city in the newly formed Confederacy. In April 1861, the Civil War began.

Although New Orleans was protected by Fort Jackson and Fort St. Philip on the Mississippi River, approximately seventy-five miles below the city, this protection proved to be inadequate. In March of 1862, after five days and nights of artillery bombardment, a Union fleet of warships and mortar boats managed to maneuver past the Confederate barricade, overcome a Confederate defense fleet, and continue upriver. They arrived in New Orleans on April 15.

Reinforced by 18,000 troops, Gen. Benjamin Butler took control of the city, ushering in the federal occupation that would last for the next fifteen years. Combined with the abolition of slavery, the era of Reconstruction, and the loss of river trade, the flamboyant life of antebellum New Orleans came to an end.

The Civil War took its toll on New Orleans, and in the decades that followed, the city's importance as a commercial center drastically declined—the city was impoverished. It was a time of violence, lawlessness, and corruption.

REBUILDING THE CITY

Eventually, as America regrouped in the aftermath of the war, the economy of New Orleans began to rebound. The expansion of railroads in the North, which had been accelerated by the war, had drastically decreased river trade. In an effort to stimulate economic growth, political leaders rebuilt much of the city's port, and their efforts proved successful, as before long, construction activity began to increase and the city's economy began to bounce back.

The cotton trade with Europe and New England expanded, and a new agricultural trade developed with Latin America, primarily because of the city's strategic location. Irish and German immigrants continued to migrate to New Orleans and were soon joined by the Italians. By 1878 the population of New Orleans had reached 210,000.

The Indian presence was still evident in the Quarter; during the 1880s, fifteen to twenty Choctaw women (their features showing the signs of generations of intermarriage between Indians and Africans) spread their wares in the French Market on Wednesdays and in Jackson Square on Saturdays, a tradition that continued until the 1920s. The Indians disappeared in New Orleans, not because they died out or moved away, but because, in the words of an 1880s observer, they "melted away into mulattoes." The Indians became New Orleanians by gradually blending into the city's African community (Hirsch 1992).

First gaining recognition in America during the 1850s, the Victorian aesthetic revolved around variety and a sense of playfulness, in comparison to the seriousness of Greek Revival. By the 1860s, while maintaining its dominance longer in New Orleans than in most of the rest of the country, Greek Revival began to lose favor, and by the late 1870s, the Victorian aesthetic had risen to the forefront of architectural fashion in New Orleans. The Greek Revival era was rapidly coming to an end, gradually giving way to its ornamented sister, the Italianate style.

The Italianate style dominated the city, including the Quarter, from about 1870 to the mid-1880s, at which time the Victorian drive for variety in texture and ornament increased, and the last remnants of classicism were replaced by the emerging styles of Eastlake, Queen Anne, and Bracket. Ornament was now being used with reckless abandon. Steam-driven lathe and jigsaw equipment was turning out mass-produced ornamentation and sawmills were cutting timber into dimensional lumber. Turned columns, brackets, balusters, and scrollwork, as well as a variety of ornamental millwork, playful colors, and elaborate ornamentation were in evidence everywhere and Queen Anne houses sprung up with wings, bay, turrets, and multiple and varied roof forms.

In the Quarter, numerous buildings were demolished and replaced by Eastlake and Bracket-style single and double shotguns, camelbacks, and Eastlake double-gallery houses. The era waned by the turn of the century and came to an end within a few years with a return to classical ideals in the form of neoclassical and Georgian revival styles. It was the most innovative era in America's architectural history and left its imprint throughout the country. The French Quarter has numerous Victorian structures, legacies to an era in search of novelty and innovation.

BUILDING TYPES

The most common housing types constructed in the Quarter in the Victorian era were shotgun singles (as described earlier), shotgun doubles, and camelbacks.

Shotgun Houses

Shotgun single houses were described earlier in chapter four. Shotgun doubles, a variety of the type, can best be described as dwellings housing two shotgun singles under a common roof, separated by a common wall. On the common wall are fireplaces servicing two rooms, or in some cases, located at corners serving four rooms. Like shotgun singles, they consist of from three to seven rooms, arranged one behind the other with no halls, and have four-bay fenestrations—door-window-window-door. Windows located on the front facade were generally double-hung opening full length to the floor.

Camelbacks

Most likely originated in New Orleans, camelbacks are generally single or double shotgun houses with a second story located at the rear, which generally housed one or more bedrooms. Camelbacks were common in New Orleans from about 1860 to the early 1900s.

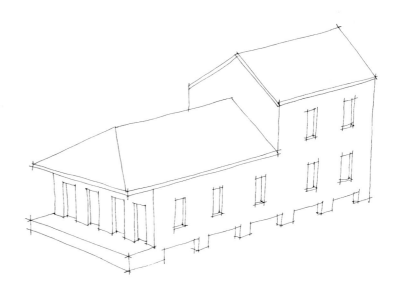

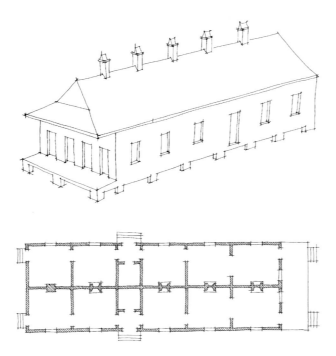

BUILDING STYLES

The Victorian era introduced a number of architectural styles in New Orleans, primarily Italianate, Second Empire, Eastlake, Bracket style, and Queen Anne. While to be found in the Quarter, examples of Second Empire and Queen Anne houses are not common.

Italianate

In the late 1850s, public sensibilities began to evolve the Greek Revival style toward a more ornate classicism. By 1860, the public taste had evolved to an appreciation of the Italianate style, a classical style with greater exuberance than that of the Greek Revival style. It owed its inspiration to the Italian renaissance. It would domi-nate the architectural scene until the early 1870s, at which time the excesses of the Victorian era abandoned the classical idioms completely and created more ornate styles. The major characteristics of the style are bracketed cornices with paired brackets in the entablature aligned over columns, ornamented columns, quoins, keystones, rustication, stilted arches, and decorative parapets.

159

Bracket Style

A style indigenous to New Orleans, Bracket style resulted from a blending of the Italianate style with the more vigorous gymnastics of Victorian sensibilities. Ornamental wooden brackets, common under the eaves of Italianate houses, were now elongated in a horizontal direction and used to support a deep overhang over the front gallery, in lieu of columns that were being used in Eastlake houses. These houses were almost always of wood frame and wood siding. Windows on the front facade opening onto the gallery, were usually double hung, two over four, and full length. Openings were either flat-topped or segmentally arched. In the French Quarter, the style is most often utilized for single and double shotgun houses.

160

Eastlake

The Eastlake style derives its name from the English architect Charles Locke Eastlake, who in 1868 wrote *Hints on Household Taste*. This book on furniture design illustrated furniture highly ornamented with turned-wood components. Capitalizing on this aesthetic, American designers created a new style. By the 1880s, the style had become popular in houses throughout America, and would remain so until the early 1900s. Envisioning his creation to be used only on furniture, Mr. Eastlake never appreciated this American phenomenon.

BRACKET-STYLE SHOTGUNS

1001/1003 and 1009 Saint Phillip Street
Circa 1890

Located at the corner of Saint Phillip and Burgundy streets, these houses are good examples of the shotgun double camelback and shotgun single. Information on their history is scarce, but as bracket-style houses, they were most likely constructed sometime around 1890.

Directly at the sidewalk and built approximately three feet above the ground on a brick, chain-wall foundation, these wood-frame houses have weatherboard siding on the sides and rear and drop siding with corner quoins on the front façade, typical of the type and style. Ornate wooden brackets support the hip roof, which projects over the front façade, protecting the front openings. The roof is gable-on-hip, and the front gable has a stained-glass window illuminating the attic.

The entry doors feature a single glass light over a wooden panel, with a transom above. Full-length windows are two-over-four, with segmentally arched tops, ornate cornices, and cast-iron railings. The houses exemplify wooden ornamentation in the Victorian era.

Lloyd Vogt

EASTLAKE SHOTGUN DOUBLE

1019/1021 Dauphine Street
Circa 1895

This Eastlake shotgun double wood-frame house is one of the most ornate Victorian houses in the Quarter. While not as popular as some earlier styles used in the Quarter, the Eastlake double is found in Victorian neighborhoods throughout the city.

True to the genre, the house is a simple, raised, rectangular box with an elaborately ornamented front porch. The front facade has a gable-on-hip roof, accentuated by slightly projecting pedimented entrances clad in fish-scale shingles and aligned with stoops abutting the sidewalks. The central gable is articulated with a tri-part stained-glass window, allowing light into the attic. Wooden entry doors with glass lights and transoms above flank two-over-four, full-length windows opening onto the porch.

The front porch makes extensive use of lathe and jigsaw work, which during the era was being mass produced by local millwork shops. Ornate, turned-wood colonnettes define the four bays, and are joined by ornamental spandrels comprised of turned spindles terminated at each side by piercework panels. Small brackets create the continuity between the spandrels and the colonnettes. The balustrade is comprised of turned-wood balusters, adding to the harmony of the ornamental ensemble.

Lloyd Vogt

THE TWENTIETH CENTURY 1900—2000

BY THE TURN OF THE CENTURY, the population of New Orleans had grown to 287,104. The economy of the city having been ravaged in the aftermath of the Civil War, the French Quarter had fallen out of favor as a place to live. Most of its inhabitants had moved to surrounding neighborhoods and many of the older structures had deteriorated badly. In their decaying condition, with accompanying low rents, they provided economically feasible housing for arriving immigrants.

The early 1900s witnessed a large number of immigrants from Sicily and southern Italy, most of whom found housing in the Quarter. Although they had limited financial resources, by occupying the structures and providing minimal maintenance, they prevented further deterioration, ultimately saving many structures from demolition. The limited finances of the Italians placed them outside of the fashionable pursuit of "remodeling," a practice that has devastated much of America's historic architecture. Fortunately, most of the structures were left unaltered.

The Italians gravitated to jobs with which they were accustomed—fishing, farming, and the selling of produce. Soon they began to dominate the French Market, becoming the principal vegetable and produce vendors. Central Grocery was opened and the muffuletta sandwich was born. As their economic status improved, they purchased buildings in the Quarter for businesses and housing and soon became the predominant inhabitants of the area surrounding the French Market.

Consequently, the French Quarter was saved from mass demolition and insensitive remodeling, and as a result, the destruction and reconstruction synonymous with turn-of-the-century progress and modernization bypassed the Quarter and took its toll on the historic structures in the American sector across Canal Street.

In 1897, in an effort to control prostitution, city alderman Sidney Story spearheaded a plan that resulted in the adoption of a city ordinance creating a restricted district for legalized prostitution. The area, centered on Basin Street on the northern edge of the Quarter, became known as Storyville, much to Alderman Story's dismay. In 1917, at the request of Josephus Daniels, U.S. Secretary of the Navy, who intended to curb the military-service personnel's accessibility to the vices of the district, Storyville was closed by a city ordinance. During twenty years of operation, the brothels of Storyville served as the venue for numerous bands who gave birth to New Orleans jazz. Out of this era came King Oliver, Louis Armstrong, Buddy Bolton, and Johnny DeDroit, among many others. In 1917, the Original Dixieland Jazz Band released "Livery Stable Blues," generally considered to be the first commercial jazz recording. As the popularity of jazz grew, bands began playing at balls, dances, picnic outings, and parades all over New Orleans.

Around the turn of the century, a Sewerage and Water Board engineer named Albert Baldwin Wood developed the screw pump, drastically improving drainage in the city, as well as providing the technology to drain the surrounding swamps. Wood's pumping system, with its network of canals, allowed for the expansion of New Orleans northward toward Lake Pontchartrain. His pumps proved to be extremely efficient. Today, there are twenty-two pumping stations in the city, with almost fifty of the original pumps still in operation.

In 1905, one of the causes of yellow fever, the *Aedes aegypti* mosquito, was discovered, prompting the construction of a municipal water purification plant, followed by the practice of screening cisterns, oiling gutters, and eventually screening houses. Another looming fear, bubonic plague, was spread by fleas common to rats, and New Orleans was rat-infested—getting the problem under control became a monumental task. A rat-proofing ordinance was adopted, strictly enforced, and paid for by a property tax. Every house was

167

inspected and hundreds of men were employed as the "rat catching brigade." The brigade's search-and-destroy mission eliminated from the city more than two million rats.

In 1910, the Louisiana State Museum opened exhibits at the Cabildo and Presbytère, and in 1913, Le Petit Theatre du Vieux Carré opened its doors. In 1916 and in 1918, the city fell victim to the flu pandemic, rapidly spreading across the nation.

Shortly after World War I, the Quarter began to experience a period of renewed interest and revitalization. Bernard Lemann tells us: "Orleanians and newcomers, chiefly artists and literary people were attracted by low rentals and by the incredible raw material for painting, drama or fiction. To the uninitiated, the glimpses of the accumulated filth, the unsightly beggars along deserted, steaming sidewalks, and at night the drunks and toughs, and insinuations whispered through shutter blinds, carried associations of something a little dangerous, if not downright improper." The Quarter provided intrigue, and coupled with an attitude that fostered creative freedom, captured countless writers, artists, and free thinkers including William Faulkner, Ernest Hemingway, Sherwood Anderson, and Tennessee Williams.

In 1908, an entire block of historic buildings between Chartres and Royal streets was demolished to construct the Civil Court buildings. At the same time, the old St. Louis Exchange Hotel, the site of the state capital in 1874, was allowed to decay and was demolished after being damaged by the hurricane of 1915. In 1921, realizing that the future of the Quarter was in peril, the Vieux Carré Commission was established, and by the state's enabling legislation of 1936 and the Vieux Carré Ordinance of 1937, was given the authority to legally protect and preserve the historic character of the Quarter.

In 1930s, President Roosevelt's WPA moved into the Quarter and began a rehabilitation program. The French Market, Jackson Square, Cathedral, Cabildo, Presbytère, and Pontalba buildings were all renovated. While the rehabilitation efforts undoubtedly stabilized the Quarter, unfortunately, many of the city's earliest structures were demolished in the process (Garvey 1982).

In the 1940s, the nightclubs in the Quarter became heavily patronized by military servicemen in port, prompting the opening of numerous clubs featuring "girlie" shows and live music. Bourbon Street became the center of the action, ultimately creating Bourbon Street as we know it today.

As tourism increased in the Quarter, so did the establishment of inns and hotels—a trend that continues to this day. In the 1944, J & M Amusements acquired the building at 838 North Rampart Street and Cosimo Matassa opened the J&M Recording Studio. Before long, the studio became ground zero for the development of the "New Orleans Sound"; the result of pioneering rhythm and blues and rock and roll recordings recorded there between 1947 and 1956 by the likes of Fats Domino, Dave Bartholomew, Professor Longhair, Smiley Lewis, Joe Turner, Guitar Slim, Shirley & Lee, Lloyd Price, Jerry Lee Lewis, Little Richard, Ray Charles, and numerous others.

In 1949, the streetcars were removed from the Quarter and replaced with buses. In 1973 Mardi Gras parades were discontinued in the Quarter for fear of fire. By 1950, the population of New Orleans had grown to 570,445 and America's fascination with the automobile was beginning to be felt in New Orleans. In 1958, the Greater New Orleans Bridge was opened and connected New Orleans with the West Bank. In 1964, the streetcars were removed from Canal Street. The American love affair with the automobile crept into the Quarter, surfacing with a planned, elevated, six-lane riverfront expressway that would have essentially created a wall separating the entire French Quarter from the river. From 1959 to 1969, a major battle was waged against the Louisiana Department of Highways by a group of concerned citizens who, realizing the pending devastation to the Quarter, formed a coalition to fight the proposal. After a long hard-fought battle, locally referred to as the "Second Battle of New Orleans," the proposal was defeated (Baumbach-Borah 1981).

With the threat of the expressway eliminated, the riverfront was opened up to pedestrians with the construction of the Moonwalk, a pedestrian riverfront overlook located adjacent to Jackson Square. In

1996, the U.S. Mint was taken over by the State of Louisiana, and in the mid-1970s, the French Market underwent a major renovation. The riverfront streetcar line became operational in 1987, and with the construction of Woldenberg Park in 1989, the Quarter recaptured a large expanse of the riverfront for the pedestrians.

However, the continual improvements and expanding commercial success of the Quarter has not come without problems; increased traffic, tourism, and conversion of residential properties to commercial establishments has continued to reduce the number of residents living in the Quarter. The delicate balance of commercial and residential is of major concern, for this balance is essential if the Quarter is to continue to thrive as a viable, living community and not become a sideshow for the entertainment of visitors.

Change is not only inevitable, but essential, and the Quarter has experienced great change since its founding in 1718. However, the task at hand is to summons the collective wisdom of the community to provide the guidance to ensure the preservation and survival, for future generations, of the unique and irreplacable sector we call the French Quarter.

EPILOGUE

After almost three centuries, the Quarter continues to be the heart of New Orleans. The cultural identity of cities derives from their histories, and the Quarter has played a major role in giving form to the identity of New Orleans. The lifestyles and values of those who have contributed to its development are everywhere in evidence. Here, the past clings to the present with reassuring comfort while continuing to shape its future.

There are great lessons to be learned from history, and the Quarter is an important example upon which to draw. The best that twentieth-century thinking and technology have been able to accomplish in the built environment pales by way of such historic places as the Quarter. Our twentieth-century culture has failed at building cities that are humane, that engage the senses, that enrich the human experience, and that are worth caring about. We have allowed convenience, economics, and the automobile to set the planning and design guidelines for most of our communities, ignoring the wisdom of history. While places such as the Quarter are internationally celebrated, we have used governmental regulations to rule out the possibility of similar places ever being built in the future. Perhaps, by better understanding our forefathers, we can better understand our failures, and once again begin to build cities that respond to human needs and emotions and enhance life's everyday experiences.

People are drawn to the Quarter for the emotional experience it provides, and judging by the numbers who come, the experience is one that reaches deep into the human psyche, fueling a range of emotions and constantly challenging the senses. Sounds, smells, and the play of sun, shade, and shadow against an incredible array of colors and textures reach us at subconscious levels and teach us wordlessly.

The Quarter possesses a sense of playfulness. It says "live for today for there may be no tomorrow"; how else could a group of people act, when for so many of their loved ones there was no tomorrow? It is tolerant to the extreme—rich to poor, pious to decadent; how else could a group of people from thirty-two countries live together and survive?

The Quarter exudes romance, mystery, and intrigue; in this regard, it has no American peer. It wears no mask. It presents to the world its attributes as well as its faults, and it makes no apologies. It seems comfortable with its identity, and in some mysterious way, encourages those who wander into it to shed their masks, to be free from the burden of social convention. Its dark side is ever-present, along with its outpouring of generosity. It welcomes, it embraces, it accepts all—it is a potpourri of the human condition, a safe haven, the mother hen of the common, the eccentric, the lost, the odd, and the indifferent.

The Quarter is blind to the concept of social status, intolerant of the intolerant, and has no expectations of those it shelters. It manifests life's extremes; it represents people at their best and at their worst, for it has experienced, and has survived, the best and the worst of life's offerings. Its mere existence is a testimony to the perseverance of the human spirit.

It is the heart and soul of the city. It is the French Quarter.

GLOSSARY

A

ARCH—A curvilinear structural opening.

B

BALCONY—A platform projecting from an upper level of a building and surrounded by a railing.

BALUSTER—A shaftlike element used to support a handrail.

BALUSTRADE—A railing (such as a porch railing) made up of rails, balusters, and posts.

BARREL TILE—A half-cylinder-shaped clay roof tile.

BATTURE—Lowlands at the river's edge, typically inundated during high water.

BAYS—Repetitive divisions into which a building is divided, such as the columns on a porch.

BOUSILLAGE—A construction method for walls using a mixture of mud and moss as infill between heavy timber posts.

C

CABINET—A small room situated in the rear outer corner of certain house types, primarily French colonial, Creole cottages, and American cottages.

CASEMENT WINDOW—A window that swings on hinges like a door; a common window type in colonial New Orleans.

CAST IRON—Iron shaped by placement in a mold, used for railing, fences, etc.

CLASSICAL ARCHITECTURE—The architecture of Greece and Rome during the pre-Christian era.

COLONNETTES—Slender, turned wooden columns.

CORINTHIAN ORDER—The most ornate of the classical Greek orders, characterized by a bell-shaped capital decorated with acanthus leaves.

CREOLE—A person descended from French and/or Spanish colonists; also used to describe a style of architecture prevalent during the postcolonial period in New Orleans.

D

DENTILS—Closely spaced blocks in Greek Ionic and Corinthian cornices.

DORIC ORDER—The simplest of the classical Greek orders, distinguished by columns with unadorned capitals and no bases.

DORMER—A projection from a wall or roof structure. When it rises from a roof, it is called a roof dormer, and when it is an extension of a wall, it is called a wall dormer.

DOUBLE-HUNG WINDOW—A window type introduced to New Orleans in the early 1800s, consisting of two sashes that operate through vertical movement.

E

EAVE—The projecting overhang of a roof.

EGG-AND-DART—Decorative molding consisting of alternating egg-and dart-shaped elements.

ENTABLATURE—In classical architecture, the horizontal part of a classical order, supported by columns or pilasters and consisting of the architrave, the frieze, and the cornice.

F

FANLIGHT—A fan-shaped or semicircular window over a door or window with radiating muntins.

FENESTRATIONS—The window and door openings in a building.

FINIAL—The topping ornament of a roof gable, turret, baluster, post, etc.

FLUTING—Closely spaced, parallel, vertical channeling on the shaft of a column or pilaster.

FRENCH DOORS—A pair of hinged doors, generally with glass lights.

G

GABLE ORNAMENT—Decorative woodwork located in the apex of a gable. (Often in conjunction with decorative barge boards.)

GALLERY—Exterior space under the main roof of a house, derived from French term *galerie*. Can be used interchangeably with porch.

GREEK KEY—An overlapping lintel over a doorway with a slight flaring-out of the face of the doorway surround from the top to the bottom.

H

HALF-TIMBERING—A method of wall construction in which the wooden structural members are exposed on the exterior wall, with stucco infill between.

HIPPED ROOF—A roof with uniformly sloped sides.

I

IONIC ORDER—An order of classical Greek architecture, characterized by columns with a scroll-like capital.

J

JIGSAW WORK—Decorative woodwork, generally curvilinear in shape, common in the Victorian era and produced by the use of a jigsaw.

L

LEADED GLASS—Small panes of glass—clear, beveled, or stained—held together by lead strips.

LIGHT—A glass pane in a window or door.

LOGGIA—A gallery enclosed on three sides, serving as an open-air room.

M

MILLWORK—Woodwork shaped or dressed by means of a rotary cutter.

MOLDING—A linear decorative element, or curved strip, used for ornamentation or trimwork.

P

PEDIMENT—A low-pitched gable in the classical manner; also used in miniature over doors or windows.

PIERCEWORK—Ornamentation common in the late Victorian period, created by cutting openings in various shapes in a solid piece of wood.

PILASTER—A column (typically half-column) attached to a wall.

PITCH—The angle or slope of a roof.

R

REGAS—Wooden grating on windows facing the street.

ROUND-HEADED WINDOW—A window whose uppermost part is rounded.

S

SASH—The wood frame of a window in which the glass panes are set.

SEMI-OCTAGONAL BAY—A projecting bay in the shape of a section of an octagon.

SHINGLES—A wall or roof covering, consisting of small overlapping pieces, square or patterned.

SHUTTER—A hinged movable cover, usually of wood, for a window or door.

SIDELIGHTS—Stationary glass panes flanking an entrance door.

SIDING—The material used to cover the exposed side of a wood-frame building (weatherboard, drop siding, etc.).

SPINDLE—A turned decorative wooden element.

SPINDLE BAND—A row of spindles included as the uppermost decorative feature of a gallery or porch below the cornice, also known as an openwork frieze.

SQUARE-HEADED WINDOW—A window whose uppermost part is horizontal, at ninety degrees to the sides.

SWAGS—Classical ornamentation resembling evergreen branches hanging in a curve between two points.

T

TRANSOM—A glazed opening over a door or window.

173

BIBLIOGRAPHY

Arthur, Stanley Clisby. *Old New Orleans*. Edited by Susan Cole Dore. 1936. Reprint, Gretna, Louisiana: Pelican Publishing Company, 1990.

Atroshenko, V. I., and Milton Grundy. *Mediterranean Vernacular: A Vanishing Architectural Tradition*. New York: Rizzoli International Publications, Inc., 1991.

Badger, Daniel D. *Badger's Illustrated Catalogue of Cast-iron Architecture*. New York: Dover Publications, Inc., 1981.

Baumbach, Richard O., Jr., and William E. Borah. *The Second Battle of New Orleans*. University, AL: University of Alabama Press, 1981.

Berthelot, Jack, and Martine Gaumé. *Kaz Antiyé Jan Moun Ka Rete. Caribbean Popular Dwelling*. Caribees :Paris Editions, 1982.

Binney, Marcus. *Townhouses: Urban Houses from 1200 to the Present Day*. New York: Whitney Library of Design, 1998.

Boorstin, Daniel J. *The Discoverers: A History of Man's Search to Know His World and Himself*. New York: Vintage Books: A Division of Random House, 1985.

Carley, Rachel. *Cuba: 400 Years of Architectural Heritage*. New York: Whitney Library of Design, 1997.

Crain, Edward E. *Historic Architecture in the Caribbean Islands*. Gainesville, FL: University Press of Florida, 1994.

Daspit, Fred. *Louisiana Architecture: 1714-1830*. Lafayette, LA: The Center for Louisiana Studies-USL, 1996.

Davis, Edwin Adams; Raleigh A. Suarez; and Joe Gray Taylor. *Louisiana: The Pelican State. (Revised Edition)*. Baton Rouge, LA: Louisiana State University Press, 1985.

Edwards, Jay D. *Louisiana's Remarkable French Vernacular Architecture*. Baton Rouge, LA: Geoscience Publications (LSU), 1988.

_____. "The Origins of Creole Architecture." in *Winterthur Portfolio*. Vol. 29:2-3, 1994.

Edwards, Jay D. "Cultural Identifications in Architecture: The Case of the New Orleans Townhouse." *Traditional Dwellings and Settlements Review*, vol. V, no. I (Fall 1993).

_____. "What Louisiana Architecture Owes to Hispañola." *Louisiana Cultural Vistas*. New Orleans: Endowment for the Humanities, Summer, 1999.

Faucon, Régis, and Yves Lescroart. *Manor Houses in Normandy*. Koln: Konemann Verlagsgesellschaft mbH, 1997.

Fragner, Benjamin. *The Illustrated History of Architecture: The Development of Cities and Towns*. London: Sunburst Books, 1994.

Garvey, Joan, and Mary Lou Widmer. *Beautiful Crescent: A History of New Orleans*. New Orleans: Garmer Press, 1982.

Gayaree, Charles. *History of Louisiana, Vol. 3, 3rd Ed*. New Orleans: Arm and Hawkins, 1885.

Gayle, Margot, and Carol Gayle. *Cast-Iron Architecture in America*. New York: W. W. Norton & Company, 1998.

Geerlings, Gerald K. *Wrought Iron in Architecture: An Illustrated Survey*. 1929. Reprint, New York: Dover Publications, 1983.

Glassie, Henry. *Pattern in the Material Folk Culture of the Eastern United States*. Philadelphia: University of Pennsylvania Press, 1968.

Gurtner, George, and Frank Methe. *Historic Churches of Old New Orleans*. New Orleans: Friends of St. Alphonsus, 1996.

Hanger, Kimberly S. *Bounded Lives, Bounded Places: Free Black Society in Colonial New Orleans, 1769-1803*. Durham & London: Duke University Press, 1997.

Haring, C. H. *The Spanish Empire in America*. 1947. Reprint, Harcourt Brace Jovanovich Publishers, 1952.

Harris, Cyril M. *Illustrated Dictionary of Historic Architecture*. 1977. Reprint, New York: Dove Publications, 1983.

Hauck, Philomena. *Bienville: Father of Louisiana*. Lafayette, LA: University of Southwestern Louisiana-The Center for Louisiana Studies, 1998.

Heard, Malcolm. *French Quarter Manual*. New Orleans: Tulane School of Architecture, 1997.

Heck, Robert W., and Otis B. Wheeler. *Religious Architecture in*

Louisiana. Baton Rouge, LA: Louisiana State University Press, 1995.

Hirsch, Arnold R., and Joseph Logsdon. *Creole New Orleans: Race and Americanization*. Baton Rouge, LA: Louisiana State University Press, 1992.

Huber, Leonard V. *Landmarks of New Orleans*. New Orleans: Louisiana Landmarks Society and Orleans Parish Landmarks Commission, 1984.

_____; and Peggy McDowell; and Mary Louise Christovich. *New Orleans Architecture: Volume III, The Cemeteries*. Gretna, LA: Pelican Publishing Company, 1997.

Kniffen, Fred B. "Folk Housing: Key to Diffusion" *Annals of the Association of American Geographers*, vol. LV, no. 4 (December, 1965).

Kniffen, Fred B., and Henry Glassie. *Building in Wood in the Eastern United States: A Time-Place Perspective*. Athens, GA: University of Georgia Press, 1986.

Lane, Mills. *Architecture of the Old South: Louisiana*. Savannah, GA: The Beehive Foundation, 1990.

Laws, Bill. *Rural Spain*. New York: Abbeville Press, 1995.

_____. *Rural France*. New York: Abbeville Press, 1991.

Leavitt, Mel. *A Short History of New Orleans*. San Francisco: Lexikos, 1982.

Lemann, Bernard. *The Vieux Carré—A General Statement*. New Orleans: Tulane University School of Architecture, 1966.

Llanes, Lilian. *The Houses of Old Cuba*. New York: Thames & Hudson, 1999.

Manucy, Albert. *The Houses of St. Augustine 565-1821*. St. Augustine, FL: The St. Augustine Historical Society, 1978.

Masson, Ann M., and Lydia H. L. Schmalz. *Cast Iron and the Crescent City*. New Orleans: Louisiana Landmarks Society, 1995.

McDermott, John Francis, ed. *Frenchmen and French Ways in the Mississippi Valley*. Urbana, IL: University of Illinois Press, 1969.

McWilliams, Richebourg Gaillard. *Iberville's Gulf Journals*. University, AL: University of Alabama Press, 1981.

Mumford, Lewis. *The City in History: Its Origins, Its Transformations, and its Prospects*. New York: MJF Books, 1961.

Newton, Milton B., Jr. *Atlas of Louisiana: A Guide for Students*. Baton Rouge, LA: Louisiana State University, 1972.

_____. *Louisiana Geography: A Syllabus*. Baton Rouge, LA: Louisiana State University, 1976.

_____. "Louisiana House Types: A Field Guide." *Melanges*, No. 2 (September 27, 1971).

Oliver, Paul. *Dwellings: The House Across the World*. Austin: University of Texas Press, 1990.

Parkerson, Codman. *New Orleans: America's Most Fortified City*. New Orleans: The Quest, 1991

Pevsner, Nikolaus. *An Outline of European Architecture*. Middlesex, England: Penguin Books, Ltd. Harmondsworth, 1943.

Phelps, Albert. *Louisiana: A Record of Expansion*. Boston: Houghton, Mifflin, and Company, 1905.

Poesch, Jessie, and Barbara SoRelle Bacot, eds. *Louisiana Buildings, 1720-1940: The Historic American Buildings Survey*. Baton Rouge, LA: Louisiana State University Press, 1997.

Quiney, Anthony. *The Traditional Buildings of England*. New York: Thames and Hudson Inc., 1990.

Revello, Jose Torre. *Catalogue de Mapas y Planos*. Archivo General de Indias: Ministero de Cultura, 1988.

Risebero, Bill. *The Story of Western Architecture*. Cambridge, MA: MIT Press, 1985.

Rogozinski, Jan. *A Brief History of the Caribbean*. New York: Meridian-Penguin Group, 1992.

Saxon, Lyle. *Fabulous New Orleans*. 1928. Reprint, Gretna, LA: Pelican Publishing Company, 1988.

Scroggs, William O. *The Story of Louisiana*. Indianapolis: Bobbs-Merril Company, 1924.

Segre, Roberto; Mario Coyula; and Joseph L. Scarpaci. *Havana: Two Faces of the Antillean Metropolis*. West Sussex, England: John Wiley & Sons, 1997.

Slesin, Suzanne; Stafford Cliff; Jack Berthelot; Martine Gaumé; and

Daniel Rozensztroch. *Caribbean Style*. New York: Clarkson N. Potter, Inc., 1985.

Spitzer, Nicholas. "Cajuns and Creoles: The French Gulf Coast." *Southern Exposure* (Summer/fall 1977).

Street-Porter, Tim. *Mexicana*. New York: Stewart, Tabori & Chang, Inc., 1989.

Strout, Nancy, and Jorge Rigau. *Havana*. New York: Rizzoli International Publications, Inc., 1994.

Sullivan, Charles L. *The Mississippi Gulf Coast: Portrait of a People*. Northridge, CA: Windsor Publications, Inc., 1985.

Sutcliffe, Anthony. *Paris: An Architectural History*. New Haven and London: Yale University Press, 1993.

Toledano, Roulhac. *The National Trust Guide to New Orleans*. New York: John Wiley and Sons, Inc., 1996.

Tregle, Joseph G. Jr. "Creoles and Americans," *Creole New Orleans: Race and Americanization*. Baton Rouge, LA: Louisiana State University Press, 1992.

Upton, Dell, ed. *America's Architectural Roots: Ethnic Groups that Built America*. Washington, D.C.: Preservation Press, National Trust for Historic Preservation, 1986.

Upton, Dell, and John Michael Vlach. *Common Places: Readings in American Vernacular Architecture*. Athens and London: University of Georgia Press, 1986.

Villegas, Benjamin; German Tellez; and Antonio Casteñeda. *Casa de Hacienda: Architecture in the Colombian Countryside*. Bogota, D.C. Colombia: Villegas Editores, 1997.

Vlach, John Michael. "Sources of the Shotgun House: African and Caribbean Antecedents for Afro-American Architecture." Ph.D. diss., Indiana University, 1975.

Vogt, Lloyd. *New Orleans Houses: A House-watcher's Guide*. Gretna, LA: Pelican Publishing Company, 1985.

Wilson, Samuel, Jr. *A Guide to Architecture of New Orleans 1699-1959*. Reprint, New Orleans: Louisiana Landmarks Society, 1998
_____. *The Architecture of Colonial Louisiana* Compiled and edited by Jean M. Farnsworth and Ann M. Masson. Lafayette, LA: The Center for Louisiana Studies, University of Southwestern Louisiana, 1987.

Wilson, Samuel, Jr. *Bienville's New Orleans: A French Colonial Capital, 1718-1768*. New Orleans: Friends of the Cabildo, 1968.
_____. *The Beauregard-Keyes House*. New Orleans: The Keyes Foundation, 1993.

Wychereley, R. E. *How the Greeks Built Cities*. New York: W.W. Norton & Company, Inc., 1976.